Introduction: Stopping to Buy SparkNotes on a Snowy Evening

Whose words these are you *think* you know.
Your paper's due tomorrow, though;
We're glad to see you stopping here
To get some help before you go.

Lost your course? You'll find it here.
Face tests and essays without fear.
Between the words, good grades at stake:
Get great results throughout the year.

Once school bells caused your heart to quake
As teachers circled each mistake.
Use SparkNotes and no longer weep,
Ace every single test you take.

Yes, books are lovely, dark, and deep,
But only what you grasp you keep,
With hours to go before you sleep,
With hours to go before you sleep.

HEART OF DARKNESS

EDITORIAL DIRECTOR Laurie Barnett
DIRECTOR OF TECHNOLOGY Tammy Hepps

SERIES EDITOR John Crowther
MANAGING EDITOR Vincent Janoski

WRITERS Brian Gatten, Melissa Martin
EDITORS Patrick Flanagan, John Crowther

This edition published by Spark Publishing

Spark Publishing
A Division of SparkNotes LLC
120 Fifth Avenue, 8th Floor
New York, NY 10011

Please submit all comments and questions or report errors to www.sparknotes.com/errors

Printed and bound in the United States

ISBN 1-58663-367-8

Contents

Context

J OSEPH CONRAD DID NOT BEGIN TO LEARN ENGLISH until he was twenty-one years old. He was born Jozef Teodor Konrad Korzeniowski on December 3, 1857, in the Polish Ukraine. When Conrad was quite young, his father was exiled to Siberia on suspicion of plotting against the Russian government. After the death of the boy's mother, Conrad's father sent him to his mother's brother in Kraków to be educated, and Conrad never again saw his father. He traveled to Marseilles when he was seventeen and spent the next twenty years as a sailor. He signed on to an English ship in 1878, and eight years later he became a British subject. In 1889, he began his first novel, *Almayer's Folly,* and began actively searching for a way to fulfill his boyhood dream of traveling to the Congo. He took command of a steamship in the Belgian Congo in 1890, and his experiences in the Congo came to provide the outline for *Heart of Darkness.* Conrad's time in Africa wreaked havoc on his health, however, and he returned to England to recover. He returned to sea twice before finishing *Almayer's Folly* in 1894 and wrote several other books, including one about Marlow called *Youth: A Narrative* before beginning *Heart of Darkness* in 1898. He wrote most of his other major works—including *Lord Jim,* which also features Marlow, *Nostromo,* and *The Secret Agent,* as well as several collaborations with Ford Madox Ford—during the following two decades. Conrad died in 1924.

Conrad's works, *Heart of Darkness* in particular, provide a bridge between Victorian values and the ideals of modernism. Like their Victorian predecessors, these novels rely on traditional ideas of heroism, which are nevertheless under constant attack in a changing world and in places far from England. Women occupy traditional roles as arbiters of domesticity and morality, yet they are almost never present in the narrative; instead, the concepts of "home" and "civilization" exist merely as hypocritical ideals, meaningless to men for whom survival is in constant doubt. While the threats that Conrad's characters face are concrete ones—illness, violence, conspiracy—they nevertheless acquire a philosophical character. Like much of the best modernist literature produced in the early decades of the twentieth century, *Heart of Darkness* is as much about alienation, confusion, and profound doubt as it is about imperialism.

I

2 ❋ JOSEPH CONRAD

Imperialism is nevertheless at the center of *Heart of Darkness*. By the 1890s, most of the world's "dark places" had been placed at least nominally under European control, and the major European powers were stretched thin, trying to administer and protect massive, far-flung empires. Cracks were beginning to appear in the system: riots, wars, and the wholesale abandonment of commercial enterprises all threatened the white men living in the distant corners of empires. Things were clearly falling apart. *Heart of Darkness* suggests that this is the natural result when men are allowed to operate outside a social system of checks and balances: power, especially power over other human beings, inevitably corrupts. At the same time, this begs the question of whether it is possible to call an individual insane or wrong when he is part of a system that is so thoroughly corrupted and corrupting. *Heart of Darkness,* thus, at its most abstract level, is a narrative about the difficulty of understanding the world beyond the self, about the ability of one man to judge another.

Although *Heart of Darkness* was one of the first literary texts to provide a critical view of European imperial activities, it was initially read by critics as anything but controversial. While the book was generally admired, it was typically read either as a condemnation of a certain type of adventurer who could easily take advantage of imperialism's opportunities, or else as a sentimental novel reinforcing domestic values: Kurtz's Intended, who appears at the novella's conclusion, was roundly praised by turn-of-the-century reviewers for her maturity and sentimental appeal. Conrad's decision to set the book in a Belgian colony and to have Marlow work for a Belgian trading concern made it even easier for British readers to avoid seeing themselves reflected in *Heart of Darkness*. Although these early reactions seem ludicrous to a modern reader, they reinforce the novella's central themes of hypocrisy and absurdity.

PLOT OVERVIEW

HEART OF DARKNESS centers around Marlow, an introspective sailor, and his journey up the Congo River to meet Kurtz, reputed to be an idealistic man of great abilities. Marlow takes a job as a riverboat captain with the Company, a Belgian concern organized to trade in the Congo. As he travels to Africa and then up the Congo, Marlow encounters widespread inefficiency and brutality in the Company's stations. The native inhabitants of the region have been forced into the Company's service, and they suffer terribly from overwork and ill treatment at the hands of the Company's agents. The cruelty and squalor of imperial enterprise contrasts sharply with the impassive and majestic jungle that surrounds the white man's settlements, making them appear to be tiny islands amidst a vast darkness.

Marlow arrives at the Central Station, run by the general manager, an unwholesome, conspiratorial character. He finds that his steamship has been sunk and spends several months waiting for parts to repair it. His interest in Kurtz grows during this period. The manager and his favorite, the brickmaker, seem to fear Kurtz as a threat to their position. Kurtz is rumored to be ill, making the delays in repairing the ship all the more costly. Marlow eventually gets the parts he needs to repair his ship, and he and the manager set out with a few agents (whom Marlow calls pilgrims because of their strange habit of carrying long, wooden staves wherever they go) and a crew of cannibals on a long, difficult voyage up the river. The dense jungle and the oppressive silence make everyone aboard a little jumpy, and the occasional glimpse of a native village or the sound of drums work the pilgrims into a frenzy.

Marlow and his crew come across a hut with stacked firewood, together with a note saying that the wood is for them but that they should approach cautiously. Shortly after the steamer has taken on the firewood, it is surrounded by a dense fog. When the fog clears, the ship is attacked by an unseen band of natives, who fire arrows from the safety of the forest. The African helmsman is killed before Marlow frightens the natives away with the ship's steam whistle. Not long after, Marlow and his companions arrive at Kurtz's Inner Station, expecting to find him dead, but a half-crazed Russian trader, who meets them as they come ashore, assures them that everything is fine and informs them that he is the one who left the wood. The Russian claims that Kurtz has enlarged his mind and cannot be subjected to the same moral judgments as normal people. Apparently, Kurtz has established himself as a god with the natives and has gone on brutal raids in the surrounding territory in search of ivory. The collection of severed heads adorning the fence posts around the station attests to his "methods." The pilgrims bring Kurtz out of the station-house on a stretcher, and a large group of native warriors pours out of the forest and surrounds them. Kurtz speaks to them, and the natives disappear into the woods.

The manager brings Kurtz, who is quite ill, aboard the steamer. A beautiful native woman, apparently Kurtz's mistress, appears on the shore and stares out at the ship. The Russian implies that she is somehow involved with Kurtz and has caused trouble before through her influence over him. The Russian reveals to Marlow, after swearing him to secrecy, that Kurtz had ordered the attack on the steamer to make them believe he was dead in order that they might turn back and leave him to his plans. The Russian then leaves by canoe, fearing the displeasure of the manager. Kurtz disappears in the night, and Marlow goes out in search of him, finding him crawling on all fours toward the native camp. Marlow stops him and convinces him to return to the ship. They set off down the river the next morning, but Kurtz's health is failing fast.

Marlow listens to Kurtz talk while he pilots the ship, and Kurtz entrusts Marlow with a packet of personal documents, including an eloquent pamphlet on civilizing the savages which ends with a scrawled message that says, "Exterminate all the brutes!" The steamer breaks down, and they have to stop for repairs. Kurtz dies, uttering his last words—"The horror! The horror!"—in the presence of the confused Marlow. Marlow falls ill soon after and barely survives. Eventually he returns to Europe and goes to see Kurtz's Intended (his fiancée). She is still in mourning, even though it has been over a year since Kurtz's death, and she praises him as a paragon of virtue and achievement. She asks what his last words were, but Marlow cannot bring himself to shatter her illusions with the truth. Instead, he tells her that Kurtz's last word was her name.

CHARACTER LIST

Marlow   The protagonist of *Heart of Darkness*. Marlow is philosophical, independent-minded, and generally skeptical of those around him. He is also a master storyteller, eloquent and able to draw his listeners into his tale. Although Marlow shares many of his fellow Europeans' prejudices, he has seen enough of the world and has encountered enough debased white men to make him skeptical of imperialism.

Kurtz   The chief of the Inner Station and the object of Marlow's quest. Kurtz is a man of many talents—we learn, among other things, that he is a gifted musician and a fine painter—the chief of which are his charisma and his ability to lead men. Kurtz is a man who understands the power of words, and his writings are marked by an eloquence that obscures their horrifying message. Although he remains an enigma even to Marlow, Kurtz clearly exerts a powerful influence on the people in his life. His downfall seems to be a result of his willingness to ignore the hypocritical rules that govern European colonial conduct: Kurtz has "kicked himself loose of the earth" by fraternizing excessively with the natives and not keeping up appearances; in so doing, he has become wildly successful but has also incurred the wrath of his fellow white men.

General Manager   The chief agent of the Company in its African territory, who runs the Central Station. He owes his success to a hardy constitution that allows him to outlive all his competitors. He is average in appearance and unremarkable in abilities, but he possesses a strange capacity to produce uneasiness in those around him, keeping everyone sufficiently unsettled for him to exert his control over them.

Brickmaker The brickmaker, whom Marlow also meets at the Central Station, is a favorite of the manager and seems to be a kind of corporate spy. He never actually produces any bricks, as he is supposedly waiting for some essential element that is never delivered. He is petty and conniving and assumes that other people are, too.

Chief Accountant An efficient worker with an incredible habit of dressing up in spotless whites and keeping himself absolutely tidy despite the squalor and heat of the Outer Station, where he lives and works. He is one of the few colonials who seems to have accomplished anything: he has trained a native woman to care for his wardrobe.

Pilgrims The bumbling, greedy agents of the Central Station. They carry long wooden staves with them everywhere, reminding Marlow of traditional religious travelers. They all want to be appointed to a station so that they can trade for ivory and earn a commission, but none of them actually takes any effective steps toward achieving this goal. They are obsessed with keeping up a veneer of civilization and proper conduct, and are motivated entirely by self-interest. They hate the natives and treat them like animals, although in their greed and ridiculousness they appear less than human themselves.

Cannibals Natives hired as the crew of the steamer, a surprisingly reasonable and well-tempered bunch. Marlow respects their restraint and their calm acceptance of adversity. The leader of the group, in particular, seems to be intelligent and capable of ironic reflection upon his situation.

Russian trader A Russian sailor who has gone into the African interior as the trading representative of a Dutch company. He is boyish in appearance and temperament, and seems to exist wholly on the glamour of youth and the audacity of adventurousness. His brightly patched clothes remind Marlow of a harlequin. He is a devoted disciple of Kurtz's.

Helmsman A young man from the coast trained by Marlow's predecessor to pilot the steamer. He is a serviceable pilot, although Marlow never comes to view him as much more than a mechanical part of the boat. He is killed when the steamer is attacked by natives hiding on the riverbanks.

Kurtz's African mistress A fiercely beautiful woman loaded with jewelry who appears on the shore when Marlow's steamer arrives at and leaves the Inner Station. She seems to exert an undue influence over both Kurtz and the natives around the station, and the Russian trader points her out as someone to fear. Like Kurtz, she is an enigma: she never speaks to Marlow, and he never learns anything more about her.

Kurtz's Intended Kurtz's naive and long-suffering fiancée, whom Marlow goes to visit after Kurtz's death. Her unshakable certainty about Kurtz's love for her reinforces Marlow's belief that women live in a dream world, well insulated from reality.

Aunt Marlow's doting relative, who secures him a position with the Company. She believes firmly in imperialism as a charitable activity that brings civilization and religion to suffering, simple savages. She, too, is an example for Marlow of the naïveté and illusions of women.

The men aboard the Nellie Marlow's friends, who are with him aboard a ship on the Thames at the story's opening. They are the audience for the central story of *Heart of Darkness*, which Marlow narrates. All have been sailors at one time or another, but all now have important jobs ashore and have settled into middle-class, middle-aged lives. They represent the kind of man Marlow would have likely become had he not gone to Africa: well meaning and moral but ignorant as to a large part of the world beyond England. The narrator in particular seems to be shaken by Marlow's story. He repeatedly comments on its obscurity and Marlow's own mysterious nature.

Fresleven Marlow's predecessor as captain of the steamer. Fresleven, by all accounts a good-tempered, nonviolent man, was killed in a dispute over some hens, apparently after striking a village chief.

ANALYSIS OF MAJOR CHARACTERS

MARLOW

Although Marlow appears in several of Conrad's other works, it is important not to view him as merely a surrogate for the author. Marlow is a complicated man who anticipates the figures of high modernism while also reflecting his Victorian predecessors. Marlow is in many ways a traditional hero: tough, honest, an independent thinker, a capable man. Yet he is also "broken" or "damaged," like T. S. Eliot's J. Alfred Prufrock or William Faulkner's Quentin Compson. The world has defeated him in some fundamental way, and he is weary, skeptical, and cynical. Marlow also mediates between the figure of the intellectual and that of the "working tough." While he is clearly intelligent, eloquent, and a natural philosopher, he is not saddled with the angst of centuries' worth of Western thought. At the same time, while he is highly skilled at what he does—he repairs and then ably pilots his own ship—he is no mere manual laborer. Work, for him, is a distraction, a concrete alternative to the posturing and excuse-making of those around him.

Marlow can also be read as an intermediary between the two extremes of Kurtz and the Company. He is moderate enough to allow the reader to identify with him, yet open-minded enough to identify at least partially with either extreme. Thus, he acts as a guide for the reader. Marlow's intermediary position can be seen in his eventual illness and recovery. Unlike those who truly confront or at least acknowledge Africa and the darkness within themselves, Marlow does not die, but unlike the Company men, who focus only on money and advancement, Marlow suffers horribly. He is thus "contaminated" by his experiences and memories, and, like Coleridge's Ancient Mariner, destined, as purgation or penance, to repeat his story to all who will listen.

KURTZ

Kurtz, like Marlow, can be situated within a larger tradition. Kurtz resembles the archetypal "evil genius": the highly gifted but ultimately degenerate individual whose fall is the stuff of legend. Kurtz is related to figures like Faustus, Satan in Milton's *Paradise Lost,* *Moby-Dick*'s Ahab, and *Wuthering Heights*'s Heathcliff. Like these characters, he is significant both for his style and eloquence and for his grandiose, almost megalomaniacal scheming. In a world of mundanely malicious men and "flabby devils," attracting enough attention to be worthy of damnation is indeed something. Kurtz can be criticized in the same terms that *Heart of Darkness* is sometimes criticized: style entirely overrules substance, providing a justification for amorality and evil.

In fact, it can be argued that style does not just override substance but actually masks the fact that Kurtz is utterly lacking in substance. Marlow refers to Kurtz as "hollow" more than once. This could be taken negatively, to mean that Kurtz is not worthy of contemplation. However, it also points to Kurtz's ability to function as a "choice of nightmares" for Marlow: in his essential emptiness, he becomes a cipher, a site upon which other things can be projected. This emptiness should not be read as benign, however, just as Kurtz's eloquence should not be allowed to overshadow the malice of his actions. Instead, Kurtz provides Marlow with a set of paradoxes that Marlow can use to evaluate himself and the Company's men.

Indeed, Kurtz is not so much a fully realized individual as a series of images constructed by others for their own use. As Marlow's visits with Kurtz's cousin, the Belgian journalist, and Kurtz's fiancée demonstrate, there seems to be no true Kurtz. To his cousin, he was a great musician; to the journalist, a brilliant politician and leader of men; to his fiancée, a great humanitarian and genius. All of these contrast with Marlow's version of the man, and he is left doubting the validity of his memories. Yet Kurtz, through his charisma and larger-than-life plans, remains with Marlow and with the reader.

THEMES, MOTIFS & SYMBOLS

THEMES

Themes are the fundamental and often universal ideas explored in a literary work.

THE HYPOCRISY OF IMPERIALISM

Heart of Darkness explores the issues surrounding imperialism in complicated ways. As Marlow travels from the Outer Station to the Central Station and finally up the river to the Inner Station, he encounters scenes of torture, cruelty, and near-slavery. At the very least, the incidental scenery of the book offers a harsh picture of colonial enterprise. The impetus behind Marlow's adventures, too, has to do with the hypocrisy inherent in the rhetoric used to justify imperialism. The men who work for the Company describe what they do as "trade," and their treatment of native Africans is part of a benevolent project of "civilization." Kurtz, on the other hand, is open about the fact that he does not trade but rather takes ivory by force, and he describes his own treatment of the natives with the words "suppression" and "extermination": he does not hide the fact that he rules through violence and intimidation. His perverse honesty leads to his downfall, as his success threatens to expose the evil practices behind European activity in Africa.

However, for Marlow as much as for Kurtz or for the Company, Africans in this book are mostly objects: Marlow refers to his helmsman as a piece of machinery, and Kurtz's African mistress is at best a piece of statuary. It can be argued that *Heart of Darkness* participates in an oppression of nonwhites that is much more sinister and much harder to remedy than the open abuses of Kurtz or the Company's men. Africans become for Marlow a mere backdrop, a human screen against which he can play out his philosophical and existential struggles. Their existence and their exoticism enable his self-contemplation. This kind of dehumanization is harder to identify than colonial violence or open racism. While *Heart of Darkness* offers a powerful condemnation of the hypocritical operations of imperialism, it also presents a set of issues surrounding race that is ultimately more troubling.

MADNESS AS A RESULT OF IMPERIALISM

Madness is closely linked to imperialism in this book. Africa is responsible for mental disintegration as well as for physical illness. Madness has two primary functions. First, it serves as an ironic device to engage the reader's sympathies. Kurtz, Marlow is told from the beginning, is mad. However, as Marlow, and the reader, begin to form a more complete picture of Kurtz, it becomes apparent that his madness is only relative, that in the context of the Company insanity is difficult to define. Thus, both Marlow and the reader begin to sympathize with Kurtz and view the Company with suspicion. Madness also functions to establish the necessity of social fictions. Although social mores and explanatory justifications are shown throughout *Heart of Darkness* to be utterly false and even leading to evil, they are nevertheless necessary for both group harmony and individual security. Madness, in *Heart of Darkness*, is the result of being removed from one's social context and allowed to be the sole arbiter of one's own actions. Madness is thus linked not only to absolute power and a kind of moral genius but to man's fundamental fallibility: Kurtz has no authority to whom he answers but himself, and this is more than any one man can bear.

THE ABSURDITY OF EVIL

This novella is, above all, an exploration of hypocrisy, ambiguity, and moral confusion. It explodes the idea of the proverbial choice between the lesser of two evils. As the idealistic Marlow is forced to align himself with either the hypocritical and malicious colonial bureaucracy or the openly malevolent, rule-defying Kurtz, it becomes increasingly clear that to try to judge either alternative is an act of folly: how can moral standards or social values be relevant in judging evil? Is there such thing as insanity in a world that has already gone insane? The number of ridiculous situations Marlow witnesses act as reflections of the larger issue: at one station, for instance, he sees a man trying to carry water in a bucket with a large hole in it. At the Outer Station, he watches native laborers blast away at a hillside with no particular goal in mind. The absurd involves both insignificant silliness and life-or-death issues, often simultaneously. That the serious and the mundane are treated similarly suggests a profound moral confusion and a tremendous hypocrisy: it is terrifying that Kurtz's homicidal megalomania and a leaky bucket provoke essentially the same reaction from Marlow.

MOTIFS

Motifs are recurring structures, contrasts, or literary devices that can help to develop and inform the text's major themes.

OBSERVATION AND EAVESDROPPING
Marlow gains a great deal of information by watching the world around him and by overhearing others' conversations, as when he listens from the deck of the wrecked steamer to the manager of the Central Station and his uncle discussing Kurtz and the Russian trader. This phenomenon speaks to the impossibility of direct communication between individuals: information must come as the result of chance observation and astute interpretation. Words themselves fail to capture meaning adequately, and thus they must be taken in the context of their utterance. Another good example of this is Marlow's conversation with the brickmaker, during which Marlow is able to figure out a good deal more than simply what the man has to say.

INTERIORS AND EXTERIORS
Comparisons between interiors and exteriors pervade *Heart of Darkness*. As the narrator states at the beginning of the text, Marlow is more interested in surfaces, in the surrounding aura of a thing rather than in any hidden nugget of meaning deep within the thing itself. This inverts the usual hierarchy of meaning: normally one seeks the deep message or hidden truth. The priority placed on observation demonstrates that penetrating to the interior of an idea or a person is impossible in this world. Thus, Marlow is confronted with a series of exteriors and surfaces—the river's banks, the forest walls around the station, Kurtz's broad forehead—that he must interpret. These exteriors are all the material he is given, and they provide him with perhaps a more profound source of knowledge than any falsely constructed interior "kernel."

DARKNESS
Darkness is important enough conceptually to be part of the book's title. However, it is difficult to discern exactly what it might mean, given that absolutely everything in the book is cloaked in darkness. Africa, England, and Brussels are all described as gloomy and some-

MOTIFS

how dark, even if the sun is shining brightly. Darkness thus seems to operate metaphorically and existentially rather than specifically. Darkness is the inability to see: this may sound simple, but as a description of the human condition it has profound implications. Failing to see another human being means failing to understand that individual and failing to establish any sort of sympathetic communion with him or her.

Symbols

Symbols are objects, characters, figures, or colors used to represent abstract ideas or concepts.

Fog
Fog is a sort of corollary to darkness. Fog not only obscures but distorts: it gives one just enough information to begin making decisions but no way to judge the accuracy of that information, which often ends up being wrong. Marlow's steamer is caught in the fog, meaning that he has no idea where he's going and no idea whether peril or open water lies ahead.

The "Whited Sepulchre"
The "whited sepulchre" is probably Brussels, where the Company's headquarters are located. A sepulchre implies death and confinement, and indeed Europe is the origin of the colonial enterprises that bring death to white men and to their colonial subjects; it is also governed by a set of reified social principles that both enable cruelty, dehumanization, and evil and prohibit change. The phrase "whited sepulchre" comes from the biblical Book of Matthew. In the passage, Matthew describes "whited sepulchres" as something beautiful on the outside but containing horrors within (the bodies of the dead); thus, the image is appropriate for Brussels, given the hypocritical Belgian rhetoric about imperialism's civilizing mission. (Belgian colonies, particularly the Congo, were notorious for the violence perpetuated against the natives.)

Women
Both Kurtz's Intended and his African mistress function as blank slates upon which the values and the wealth of their respective societies can be displayed. Marlow frequently claims that women are the keepers of naive illusions; although this sounds condemnatory, such a role is in fact crucial, as these naive illusions are at the root of

the social fictions that justify economic enterprise and colonial expansion. In return, the women are the beneficiaries of much of the resulting wealth, and they become objects upon which men can display their own success and status.

THE RIVER

The Congo River is the key to Africa for Europeans. It allows them access to the center of the continent without having to physically cross it; in other words, it allows the white man to remain always separate or outside. Africa is thus reduced to a series of two-dimensional scenes that flash by Marlow's steamer as he travels upriver. The river also seems to want to expel Europeans from Africa altogether: its current makes travel upriver slow and difficult, but the flow of water makes travel downriver, back toward "civilization," rapid and seemingly inevitable. Marlow's struggles with the river as he travels upstream toward Kurtz reflect his struggles to understand the situation in which he has found himself. The ease with which he journeys back downstream, on the other hand, mirrors his acquiescence to Kurtz and his "choice of nightmares."

SYMBOLS

Summary & Analysis

Part I

Beginning through Marlow's being hired as a steamboat captain.

Summary

At sundown, a pleasure ship called the *Nellie* lies anchored at the mouth of the Thames, waiting for the tide to go out. Five men relax on the deck of the ship: the Director of Companies, who is also the captain and host, the Lawyer, the Accountant, Marlow, and the unnamed Narrator. The five men, old friends held together by "the bond of the sea," are restless yet meditative, as if waiting for something to happen. As darkness begins to fall, and the scene becomes "less brilliant but more profound," the men recall the great men and ships that have set forth from the Thames on voyages of trade and exploration, frequently never to return. Suddenly Marlow remarks that this very spot was once "one of the dark places of the earth." He notes that when the Romans first came to England, it was a great, savage wilderness to them. He imagines what it must have been like for a young Roman captain or soldier to come to a place so far from home and lacking in comforts.

This train of thought reminds Marlow of his sole experience as a "fresh-water sailor," when as a young man he captained a steamship going up the Congo River. He recounts that he first got the idea when, after returning from a six-year voyage through Asia, he came across a map of Africa in a London shop window, which reinvigorated his childhood fantasies about the "blank spaces" on the map.

Marlow recounts how he obtained a job with the Belgian "Company" that trades on the Congo River (the Congo was then a Belgian territory) through the influence of an aunt who had friends in the Company's administration. The Company was eager to send Marlow to Africa, because one of the Company's steamer captains had recently been killed in a scuffle with the natives.

Analysis

Marlow's story of a voyage up the Congo River that he took as a young man is the main narrative of *Heart of Darkness*. Marlow's narrative is framed by another narrative, in which one of the listeners to Marlow's story explains the circumstances in which Marlow tells it. The narrator who begins *Heart of Darkness* is unnamed, as are the other three listeners, who are identified only by their professional occupations. Moreover, the narrator usually speaks in the first-person plural, describing what all four of Marlow's listeners think and feel. The unanimity and anonymity of Marlow's listeners combine to create the impression that they represent conventional perspectives and values of the British establishment.

For the narrator and his fellow travelers, the Thames conjures up images of famous British explorers who have set out from that river on glorious voyages. The narrator recounts the achievements of these explorers in a celebratory tone, calling them "knight-errants" of the sea, implying that such voyages served a sacred, higher purpose. The narrator's attitude is that these men promoted the glory of Great Britain, expanded knowledge of the globe, and contributed to the civilization and enlightenment of the rest of the planet.

At the time *Heart of Darkness* was written, the British Empire was at its peak, and Britain controlled colonies and dependencies all over the planet. The popular saying that "the sun never sets on the British Empire" was literally true. The main topic of *Heart of Darkness* is imperialism, a nation's policy of exerting influence over other areas through military, political, and economic coercion. The narrator expresses the mainstream belief that imperialism is a glorious and worthy enterprise. Indeed, in Conrad's time, "empire" was one of the central values of British subjects, the fundamental term through which Britain defined its identity and sense of purpose.

From the moment Marlow opens his mouth, he sets himself apart from his fellow passengers by conjuring up a past in which Britain was not the heart of civilization but the savage "end of the world." Likewise, the Thames was not the source of glorious journeys outward but the ominous beginning of a journey inward, into the heart of the wilderness. This is typical of Marlow as a storyteller: he narrates in an ironic tone, giving the impression that his audience's assumptions are wrong, but not presenting a clear alternative to those assumptions. Throughout his story, distinctions such as inward and outward, civilized and savage, dark and light, are called into question. But the irony of Marlow's story is not as pronounced as in a satire, and Marlow's and Conrad's attitudes regarding imperialism are never entirely clear.

From the way Marlow tells his story, it is clear that he is extremely critical of imperialism, but his reasons apparently have less to do with what imperialism does to colonized peoples than with what it does to Europeans. Marlow suggests, in the first place, that participation in imperial enterprises degrades Europeans by removing them from the "civilizing" context of European society, while simultaneously tempting them into violent behavior because of the hostility and lawlessness of the environment. Moreover, Marlow suggests that the mission of "civilizing" and "enlightening" native peoples is misguided, not because he believes that they have a viable civilization and culture already, but because they are so savage that the project is overwhelming and hopeless. Marlow expresses horror when he witnesses the violent maltreatment of the natives, and he argues that a kinship exists between black Africans and Europeans, but in the same breath he states that this kinship is "ugly" and horrifying, and that the kinship is extremely distant. Nevertheless, it is not a simple matter to evaluate whether Marlow's attitudes are conservative or progressive, racist or "enlightened."

In the first place, one would have to decide in relation to *whom* Marlow was conservative or progressive. Clearly, Marlow's story is shaped by the audience to whom he tells it. The anonymous narrator states that Marlow is unconventional in his ideas, and his listeners' derisive grunts and murmurs suggest that they are less inclined to question colonialism or to view Africans as human beings than he is. His criticisms of colonialism, both implicit and explicit, are pitched to an audience that is far more sympathetic toward the colonial enterprise than any twenty-first-century reader could be. The framing narrative puts a certain amount of distance between Marlow's narrative and Conrad himself. This framework suggests that the reader should regard Marlow ironically, but there are few cues within the text to suggest an alternative to Marlow's point of view.

PART I (CONTINUED)

Marlow's visit to the Company Headquarters through his parting with his aunt.

SUMMARY
After he hears that he has gotten the job, Marlow travels across the English Channel to a city that reminds him of a "whited sepulchre" (probably Brussels) to sign his employment contract at the Com-

pany's office. First, however, he digresses to tell the story of his predecessor with the Company, Fresleven. Much later, after the events Marlow is about to recount, Marlow was sent to recover Fresleven's bones, which he found lying in the center of a deserted African village. Despite his reputation as mild mannered, Fresleven was killed in a scuffle over some hens: after striking the village chief, he was stabbed by the chief's son. He was left there to die, and the superstitious natives immediately abandoned the village. Marlow notes that he never did find out what became of the hens.

Arriving at the Company's offices, Marlow finds two sinister women there knitting black wool, one of whom admits him to a waiting room, where he looks at a map of Africa color-coded by colonial powers. A secretary takes him into the inner office for a cursory meeting with the head of the Company. Marlow signs his contract, and the secretary takes him off to be checked over by a doctor. The doctor takes measurements of his skull, remarking that he unfortunately doesn't get to see those men who make it back from Africa. More important, the doctor tells Marlow, "the changes take place inside." The doctor is interested in learning anything that may give Belgians an advantage in colonial situations.

With all formalities completed, Marlow stops off to say goodbye to his aunt, who expresses her hope that he will aid in the civilization of savages during his service to the Company, "weaning those ignorant millions from their horrid ways." Well aware that the Company operates for profit and not for the good of humanity, and bothered by his aunt's naïveté, Marlow takes his leave of her. Before boarding the French steamer that is to take him to Africa, Marlow has a brief but strange feeling about his journey: the feeling that he is setting off for the center of the earth.

Analysis

This section has several concrete objectives. The first of these is to locate Marlow more specifically within the wider history of colonialism. It is important that he goes to Africa in the service of a Belgian company rather than a British one. The map that Marlow sees in the Company offices shows the continent overlaid with blotches of color, each color standing for a different imperial power. While the map represents a relatively neutral way of describing imperial presences in Africa, Marlow's comments about the map reveal that imperial powers were not all the same. In fact, the yellow patch— "dead in the center"—covers the site of some of the most disturbing atrocities committed in the name of empire. The Belgian king, Leopold, treated the Congo as his private treasury, and the Belgians had the reputation of being far and away the most cruel and rapacious of the colonial powers. The reference to Brussels as a "whited sepulchre" is meant to bring to mind a passage from the Book of Matthew concerning hypocrisy. The Belgian monarch spoke rhetorically about the civilizing benefits of colonialism, but the Belgian version of the practice was the bloodiest and most inhumane.

This does not, however, mean that Conrad seeks to indict the Belgians and praise other colonial powers. As Marlow journeys into the Congo, he meets men from a variety of European nations, all of whom are violent and willing to do anything to make their fortunes. Moreover, it must be remembered that Marlow himself willingly goes to work for this Belgian concern: at the moment he decides to do so, his personal desire for adventure far outweighs any concerns he might have about particular colonial practices. This section of the book also introduces another set of concerns, this time regarding women. *Heart of Darkness* has been attacked by critics as misogynistic, and there is some justification for this point of view. Marlow's aunt does express a naïvely idealistic view of the Company's mission, and Marlow is thus right to fault her for being "out of touch with truth." However, he phrases his criticism so as to make it applicable to all women, suggesting that women do not even live in the same world as men and that they must be protected from reality. Moreover, the female characters in Marlow's story are extremely flat and stylized. In part this may be because Marlow uses women symbolically as representatives of "home." Marlow associates home with ideas gotten from books and religion rather than from experience. Home is the seat of naïveté, prejudice, confinement, and oppression. It is the place of people who have not gone out into the world and experienced, and who therefore cannot understand. Nonetheless, the women in Marlow's story exert a great deal of power. The influence of Marlow's aunt does not stop at getting him the job but continues to echo through the Company's correspondence in Africa. At the Company's headquarters, Marlow encounters a number of apparently influential women, hinting that all enterprises are ultimately female-driven.

Marlow's departure from the world of Belgium and women is facilitated, according to him, by two eccentric men. The first of these is Fresleven, the story of whose death serves to build suspense and suggest to the reader the transformations that Europeans undergo in

Africa. By European standards, Fresleven was a good and gentle man, not one likely to die as he did. This means either that the European view of people is wrong and useless or else that there is something about Africa that makes men behave aberrantly. Both of these conclusions are difficult to accept practically or politically, and thus the story of Fresleven leaves the reader feeling ambivalent and cautious about Marlow's story to come.

The second figure presiding over Marlow's departure is the Company's doctor. The doctor is perhaps the ultimate symbol of futility: he uses external measurements to try to decipher what he admits are internal changes; moreover, his subjects either don't return from Africa or, if they do, don't return to see him. Thus his work and his advice are both totally useless. He is the first of a series of functionaries with pointless jobs that Marlow will encounter as he travels toward and then up the Congo River.

PART I (CONTINUED)

Marlow's journey down the coast of Africa through his meeting with the chief accountant.

SUMMARY

The French steamer takes Marlow along the coast of Africa, stopping periodically to land soldiers and customshouse officers. Marlow finds his idleness vexing, and the trip seems vaguely nightmarish to him. At one point, they come across a French man-of-war shelling an apparently uninhabited forested stretch of coast. They finally arrive at the mouth of the Congo River, where Marlow boards another steamship bound for a point thirty miles upriver. The captain of the ship, a young Swede, recognizes Marlow as a seaman and invites him on the bridge. The Swede criticizes the colonial officials and tells Marlow about another Swede who recently hanged himself on his way into the interior.

Marlow disembarks at the Company's station, which is in a terrible state of disrepair. He sees piles of decaying machinery and a cliff being blasted for no apparent purpose. He also sees a group of black prisoners walking along in chains under the guard of another black man, who wears a shoddy uniform and carries a rifle. He remarks that he had already known the "devils" of violence, greed, and desire, but that in Africa he became acquainted with the "flabby, pretending, weak-eyed devil of a rapacious and pitiless folly." Finally, Marlow comes to a grove of trees and, to his horror, finds a group of dying native laborers. He offers a biscuit to one of them; seeing a bit of white European yarn tied around his neck, he wonders at its meaning. He meets a nattily dressed white man, the Company's chief accountant (not to be confused with Marlow's friend the Accountant from the opening of the book). Marlow spends ten days here waiting for a caravan to the next station. One day, the chief accountant tells him that in the interior he will undoubtedly meet Mr. Kurtz, a first-class agent who sends in as much ivory as all the others put together and is destined for advancement. He tells Marlow to let Kurtz know that everything is satisfactory at the Outer Station when he meets him. The chief accountant is afraid to send a written message for fear it will be intercepted by undesirable elements at the Central Station.

ANALYSIS

Marlow's description of his journey on the French steamer makes use of an interior/exterior motif that continues throughout the rest of the book. Marlow frequently encounters inscrutable surfaces that tempt him to try to penetrate into the interior of situations and places. The most prominent example of this is the French man-of-war, which shells a forested wall of coastline. To Marlow's mind, the entire coastline of the African continent presents a solid green facade, and the spectacle of European guns firing blindly into that facade seems to be a futile and uncomprehending way of addressing the continent.

"The flabby, pretending, weak-eyed devil of a rapacious and pitiless folly" is one of the central images with which Marlow characterizes the behavior of the colonists. He refers back to this image at a number of key points later in the story. It is thus a very important clue as to what Marlow actually thinks is wrong about imperialism—Marlow's attitudes are usually implied rather than directly stated. Marlow distinguishes this devil from violence, greed, and desire, suggesting that the fundamental evil of imperialism is *not* that it perpetrates violence against native peoples, nor that it is motivated by greed. The flabby, weak-eyed devil seems to be distinguished above all by being shortsighted and foolish, unaware of what it is doing and ineffective.

The hand of the "flabby devil" is apparent in the travesties of administration and the widespread decay in the Company's stations. The colonials in the coastal station spend all their time blasting a cliff for no apparent reason, machinery lies broken all around, and supplies are poorly apportioned, resting in abundance where they are not needed and never sent to where they are needed. Given the level of waste and inefficiency, this kind of colonial activity clearly has something other than economic activity at stake, but just what that something might be is not apparent. Marlow's comments on the "flabby devil" produce a very ambivalent criticism of colonialism. Would Marlow approve of the violent exploitation and extortion of the Africans if it was done in a more clear-sighted and effective manner? This question is difficult to answer definitively.

On the other hand, Marlow is appalled by the ghastly, infernal spectacle of the grove of death, while the other colonials show no concern over it at all. For Marlow, the grove is the dark heart of the station. Marlow's horror at the grove suggests that the true evils of this colonial enterprise are dehumanization and death. All Marlow can offer these dying men are a few pieces of biscuit, and, despite the fact that Marlow is "not particularly tender," the situation troubles him.

In this section, Marlow finally learns the reason for the journey he is to take up the Congo, although he does not yet realize the importance this reason will later take on. The chief accountant is the first to use the name of the mysterious Mr. Kurtz, speaking of him in reverent tones and alluding to a conspiracy within the Company, the particulars of which Marlow never deciphers. Again, the name "Kurtz" provides a surface that conceals a hidden and potentially threatening situation. It is appropriate, therefore, that the chief accountant is Marlow's informant. In his dress whites, the man epitomizes success in the colonial world. His "accomplishment" lies in keeping up appearances, in looking as he would at home. Like everything else Marlow encounters, the chief accountant's surface may conceal a dark secret, in this case the native woman whom he has "taught"—perhaps violently and despite her "distaste for the work"—to care for his linens. Marlow has yet to find a single white man with a valid "excuse for being there" in Africa. More important, he has yet to understand why he himself is there.

PART I (CONTINUED)

Marlow's journey to the Central Station through the arrival of the Eldorado Exploring Expedition.

SUMMARY

Marlow travels overland for two hundred miles with a caravan of sixty men. He has one white companion who falls ill and must be carried by the native bearers, who start to desert because of the added burden. After fifteen days they arrive at the dilapidated Central Station. Marlow finds that the steamer he was to command has sunk. The general manager of the Central Station had taken the boat out two days before under the charge of a volunteer skipper, and they had torn the bottom out on some rocks. In light of what he later learns, Marlow suspects the damage to the steamer may have been intentional, to keep him from reaching Kurtz. Marlow soon meets with the general manager, who strikes him as an altogether average man who leads by inspiring an odd uneasiness in those around him and whose authority derives merely from his resistance to tropical disease. The manager tells Marlow that he took the boat out in a hurry to relieve the inner stations, especially the one belonging to Kurtz, who is rumored to be ill. He praises Kurtz as an exceptional agent and takes note that Kurtz is talked about on the coast.

> The word 'ivory' rang in the air, was whispered, was sighed. You would think they were praying to it.
> *(See* QUOTATIONS, *p.* 49*)*

Marlow sets to work dredging his ship out of the river and repairing it, which ends up taking three months. One day during this time, a grass shed housing some trade goods burns down, and the native laborers dance delightedly as it burns. One of the natives is accused of causing the fire and is beaten severely; he disappears into the forest after he recovers. Marlow overhears the manager talking with the brickmaker about Kurtz at the site of the burned hut. He enters into conversation with the brickmaker after the manager leaves, and ends up accompanying the man back to his quarters, which are noticeably more luxurious than those of the other agents. Marlow realizes after a while that the brickmaker is pumping him for information about the intentions of the Company's board of directors in Europe, about which, of course, Marlow knows nothing. Marlow notices an unusual painting on the wall, of a blindfolded woman with a lighted torch; when he asks about it, the brickmaker reveals that it is Kurtz's work.

The brickmaker tells Marlow that Kurtz is a prodigy, sent as a special emissary of Western ideals by the Company's directors and bound for quick advancement. He also reveals that he has seen confidential correspondence dealing with Marlow's appointment, from which he has construed that Marlow is also a favorite of the administration. They go outside, and the brickmaker tries to get himself into Marlow's good graces—and Kurtz's by proxy, since he believes Marlow is allied with Kurtz. Marlow realizes the brickmaker had planned on being assistant manager, and Kurtz's arrival has upset his chances. Seeing an opportunity to use the brickmaker's influence to his own ends, Marlow lets the man believe he really does have influence in Europe and tells him that he wants a quantity of rivets from the coast to repair his ship. The brickmaker leaves him with a veiled threat on his life, but Marlow enjoys his obvious distress and confusion.

Marlow finds his foreman sitting on the deck of the ship and tells him that they will have rivets in three weeks, and they both dance around exuberantly. The rivets do not come, however. Instead, the Eldorado Exploring Expedition, a group of white men intent on "tear[ing] treasure out of the bowels of the land," arrives, led by the manager's uncle, who spends his entire time at the station talking conspiratorially with his nephew. Marlow gives up on ever receiving the rivets he needs to repair his ship, and turns to wondering disinterestedly about Kurtz and his ideals.

———————————

ANALYSIS

As Marlow describes his caravan journey through the depopulated interior of the colony, he remarks ironically that he was becoming "scientifically interesting"—an allusion to his conversation with the company doctor in Brussels. Given this, it is curious that Marlow talks so little about the caravan journey itself. In part, this is because it's not directly relevant to his story—during this time he is neither in contact with representatives of the Company nor moving directly toward Kurtz. Nonetheless, something about this journey renders Marlow a mystery even to himself; he starts to think of himself as a potential case study. Africa appears to him to be something that happens to a man, without his consent. One way to interpret this is that Marlow is disowning his own responsibility (and that of his fellow employees) for the atrocities committed by the Company on the natives. Because of its merciless environment and savage inhabitants, Africa itself is responsible for colonial violence. Forced to deal with his ailing companion and a group of native porters who continually desert and abandon their loads, Marlow finds himself at the top of the proverbial slippery slope.

The men he finds at the Central Station allow him to regain his perspective, however. The goings-on here are ridiculous: for example, Marlow watches a man try to extinguish a fire using a bucket with a hole in it. The manager and the brickmaker, the men in charge, are repeatedly described as hollow, "papier-mâché" figures. For Marlow, who has just experienced the surreal horrors of the continent's interior, the idea that a man's exterior may conceal only a void is disturbing. The alternative, of course, is that at the heart of these men lies not a void but a vast, malevolent conspiracy. The machinations of the manager and the brickmaker suggest that, paradoxically, both ideas are correct: that these men indeed conceal bad intentions, but that these intentions, despite the fact that they lead to apparent evil, are meaningless in light of their context. The use of religious language to describe the agents of the Central Station reinforces this paradoxical idea. Marlow calls the Company's rank and file "pilgrims," both for their habit of carrying staves (with which to beat native laborers) and for their mindless worship of the wealth to be had from ivory.

"Ivory," as it echoes through the air of the camp, sounds to Marlow like something unreal rather than a physical substance. Marlow suggests that the word echoes because the station is only a tiny "cleared speck," surrounded by an "outside" that always threatens to close in, erasing the men and their pathetic ambitions. Over and over again in this section of the book human voices are hurled against the wilderness, only to be thrown back by the river's surface or a wall of trees. No matter how evil these men are, no matter how terrible the atrocities they commit against the natives, they are insignificant in the vastness of time and the physical world. Some critics have objected to *Heart of Darkness* on the grounds that it brushes aside or makes excuses for racism and colonial violence, and that it even glamorizes them by making them the subject of Marlow's seemingly profound ruminations.

On a more concrete level, the events of this section move Marlow ever closer to the mysterious Kurtz. Kurtz increasingly appeals to Marlow as an alternative, no matter how dire, to the repellent men around him. The painting in the brickmaker's quarters, which Marlow learns is Kurtz's work, draws Marlow in: the blindfolded woman with the torch represents for him an acknowledgment of the paradox and ambiguity of the African situation, and this is a much more sophisticated response than he has seen from any of the other Europeans he has encountered. To the reader, the painting may seem somewhat heavy-handed, with its overtly allegorical depiction of blind and unseeing European attempts to bring the "light" of civilization to Africa. Marlow, however, sees in it a level of self-awareness that offers a compelling alternative to the folly he has witnessed throughout the Company.

PART II

Marlow's overhearing of the conversation between the manager and his uncle through the beginning of his voyage up the river.

SUMMARY

One evening, as Marlow lies on the deck of his wrecked steamer, the manager and his uncle appear within earshot and discuss Kurtz. The manager complains that Kurtz has come to the Congo with plans to turn the stations into beacons of civilization and moral improvement, and that Kurtz wants to take over the manager's position. He recalls that about a year earlier Kurtz sent down a huge load of ivory of the highest quality by canoe with his clerk, but that Kurtz himself had turned back to his station after coming 300 miles down the river. The clerk, after turning over the ivory and a letter from Kurtz instructing the manager to stop sending him incompetent men, informs the manager that Kurtz has been very ill and has not completely recovered.

Continuing to converse with his uncle, the manager mentions another man whom he finds troublesome, a wandering trader. The manager's uncle tells him to go ahead and have the trader hanged, because no one will challenge his authority here. The manager's uncle also suggests that the climate may take care of all of his difficulties for him, implying that Kurtz simply may die of tropical disease. Marlow is alarmed by the apparent conspiracy between the two men and leaps to his feet, revealing himself to them. They are visibly startled but move off without acknowledging his presence. Not long after this incident, the Eldorado Expedition, led by the manager's uncle, disappears into the wilderness.

In a few days the Eldorado Expedition went into the
patient wilderness, that closed upon it as the sea closes
over a diver.

(See QUOTATIONS, p. 50)

Much later, the cryptic message arrives that all the expedition's don-keys have died. By that time, the repairs on Marlow's steamer are nearly complete, and Marlow is preparing to leave on a two-month trip up the river to Kurtz, along with the manager and several "pilgrims." The river is treacherous and the trip is difficult; the ship proceeds only with the help of a crew of natives the Europeans call cannibals, who actually prove to be quite reasonable people. The men aboard the ship hear drums at night along the riverbanks and occasionally catch glimpses of native settlements during the day, but they can only guess at what lies further inland. Marlow feels a sense of kinship between himself and the savages along the riverbanks, but his work in keeping the ship afloat and steaming keeps him safely occupied and prevents him from brooding too much.

ANALYSIS

Marlow's work ethic and professional skills are contrasted, throughout this section, with the incompetence and laziness of the Company's employees. Working to repair his ship and then piloting it up the river provides a much-needed distraction for Marlow, preventing him from brooding upon the folly of his fellow Europeans and the savagery of the natives. To Marlow's mind, work represents the fulfillment of a contract between two independent human beings. Repairing the steamer and then piloting it, he convinces himself, has little to do with the exploitation and horror he sees all around him.

Nevertheless, Marlow is continually forced to interpret the surrounding world. The description of his journey upriver is strange and disturbing. Marlow describes the trip as a journey back in time, to a "prehistoric earth." This remark reflects the European inclination to view colonized peoples as primitive, further back on the evolutionary scale than Europeans, and it recalls Marlow's comment at the beginning of his narrative about England's own past. What disturbs Marlow most about the native peoples he sees along the river, in his words, is "this suspicion of their not being inhuman": in some deep way these "savages" are like Europeans, perhaps just like the English were when

Britain was colonized by Rome. Marlow's self-imposed isolation from the manager and the rest of the pilgrims forces him to consider the African members of his crew, and he is confused about what he sees. He wonders, for example, how his native fireman (the crewman who keeps the boiler going) is any different from a poorly educated, ignorant European doing the same job.

> *It was unearthly, and the men were—No, they were not inhuman. Well, you know, that was the worst of it—the suspicion of their not being inhuman.*
>
> (*See* QUOTATIONS, *p.* 51)

The mysterious figure of Kurtz is at the heart of Marlow's confusion. The manager seems to suggest that his own resistance against the consequences of the tropical climate reflects not just physical constitution but a moral fitness, or the approval of some higher power. That this could be the case is terrifying to Marlow, and in his shock he exposes his disdain of the manager to the man himself. Yet Marlow has a difficult time analyzing what he has overheard about Kurtz: if the manager's story contains any truth, then Kurtz must be a monomaniacal if not psychotic individual. Next to the petty ambitions and sycophantic maneuverings of the manager, however, Kurtz's grandiose gestures and morally ambiguous successes are appealing.

Perhaps the most remarkable aspect of this section, though, is how little actually happens. The journey up the river is full of threatened disasters, but none of them comes to pass, thanks to Marlow's skill; the most explosive potential conflict arises from an act of eavesdropping. The stillness and silence surrounding this single steamer full of Europeans in the midst of the vast African continent provoke in Marlow an attitude of restless watchfulness: he feels as if he has "no time" and must constantly "discern, mostly by inspiration, [hidden] signs." In this way, his piloting a steamboat along a treacherous river comes to symbolize his finding his way through a world of conspiracies, mysteries, and inaccessible black faces. Now that both Africa and Europe have become impenetrable to Marlow, only the larger-than-life Kurtz seems "real."

PART II (CONTINUED)

Marlow's discovery of the stack of firewood through the attack on the steamer.

SUMMARY

Fifty miles away from Kurtz's Inner Station, the steamer sights a hut with a stack of firewood and a note that says, "Wood for you. Hurry up. Approach cautiously." The signature is illegible, but it is clearly not Kurtz's. Inside the hut, Marlow finds a battered old book on seamanship with notes in the margin in what looks like code. The manager concludes that the wood must have been left by the Russian trader, a man about whom Marlow has overheard the manager complaining. After taking aboard the firewood that serves as the ship's fuel, the party continues up the river, the steamer struggling and threatening at every moment to give out completely. Marlow ponders Kurtz constantly as they crawl along toward him.

By the evening of the second day after finding the hut, they arrive at a point eight miles from Kurtz's station. Marlow wants to press on, but the manager tells him to wait for daylight, as the waters are dangerous here. The night is strangely still and silent, and dawn brings an oppressive fog. The fog lifts suddenly and then falls again just as abruptly. The men on the steamer hear a loud, desolate cry, followed by a clamor of savage voices, and then silence again. They prepare for attack. The whites are badly shaken, but the African crewmen respond with quiet alertness. The leader of the cannibals tells Marlow matter-of-factly that his people want to eat the owners of the voices in the fog. Marlow realizes that the cannibals must be terribly hungry, as they have not been allowed to go ashore to trade for supplies, and their only food, a supply of rotting hippo meat, was long since thrown overboard by the pilgrims.

The manager authorizes Marlow to take every risk in continuing on in the fog, but Marlow refuses to do so, as they will surely ground the steamer if they proceed blindly. Marlow says he does not think the natives will attack, particularly since their cries have sounded more sorrowful than warlike. After the fog lifts, at a spot a mile and a half from the station, the natives attempt to repulse the invaders. The steamer is in a narrow channel, moving along slowly next to a high bank overgrown with bushes, when suddenly the air fills with arrows. Marlow rushes inside the pilot-house. When he leans out to close the shutter on the window, he sees that the brush is swarming with natives. Suddenly, he notices a snag in the river a short way ahead of the steamer.

The pilgrims open fire with rifles from below him, and the cloud of smoke they produce obscures his sight. Marlow's African helmsman leaves the wheel to open the shutter and shoot out with a one-shot rifle, and then stands at the open window yelling at the unseen assailants on the shore. Marlow grabs the wheel and crowds the steamer close to the bank to avoid the snag. As he does so, the helmsman takes a spear in his side and falls on Marlow's feet. Marlow frightens the attackers away by sounding the steam whistle repeatedly, and they give off a prolonged cry of fear and despair. One of the pilgrims enters the pilot-house and is shocked to see the wounded helmsman. The two white men stand over him as he dies quietly. Marlow makes the repulsed and indignant pilgrim steer while he changes his shoes and socks, which are covered in the dead man's blood. Marlow expects that Kurtz is now dead as well, and he feels a terrible disappointment at the thought.

One of Marlow's listeners breaks into his narrative at this point to comment upon the absurdity of Marlow's behavior. Marlow laughs at the man, whose comfortable bourgeois existence has never brought him into contact with anything the likes of Africa. He admits that his own behavior may have been ridiculous—he did, after all, throw a pair of brand-new shoes overboard in response to the helmsman's death—but he notes that there is something legitimate about his disappointment in thinking he will never be able to meet the man behind the legend of Kurtz.

ANALYSIS

Marlow makes a major error of interpretation in this section, when he decides that the cries coming from the riverbank do not portend an attack. That he is wrong is more or less irrelevant, since the steamer has no real ability to escape. The fog that surrounds the boat is literal and metaphorical: it obscures, distorts, and leaves Marlow with only voices and words upon which to base his judgments. Indeed, this has been Marlow's situation for much of the book, as he has had to formulate a notion of Kurtz based only on secondhand accounts of the man's exploits and personality. This has been both enriching and dangerous for Marlow. On the one hand, having the figure of Kurtz available as an object for contemplation has provided a release for Marlow, a distraction from his unsavory surroundings, and Kurtz has also functioned as a kind of blank slate onto which Marlow can project his own opinions and values. Kurtz gives Marlow a sense of possibility. At the same time, Marlow's fantasizing about Kurtz has its hazards. By becoming intrigued with Kurtz, Marlow becomes dangerously alienated from, and disliked by, the Company's representatives. Moreover, Marlow focuses his energies and hopes on a man who may be nothing like the legends surrounding him. However, with nothing else to go on and no other alternatives to the manager and his ilk, Marlow has little choice.

This section contains many instances of contradictory language, reflecting Marlow's difficult and uncomfortable position. The steamer, for example, "tears slowly along" the riverbank: "to tear" usually indicates great speed or haste, but the oxymoronic addition of "slowly" immediately strips the phrase of any discernible meaning and makes it ridiculous. Marlow's companions aboard the steamer prove equally paradoxical. The "pilgrims" are rough and violent men. The "cannibals," on the other hand, conduct themselves with quiet dignity: although they are malnourished, they perform their jobs without complaint. Indeed, they even show flashes of humor, as when their leader teases Marlow by saying that they would like to eat the owners of the voices they hear coming from the shore. The combination of humane cannibals and bloodthirsty pilgrims, all overseen by a manager who manages clandestinely rather than openly, creates an atmosphere of the surreal and the absurd. Thus, it is not surprising when the ship is attacked by Stone Age weaponry (arrows and spears), and it is equally appropriate that the attack is not repelled with bullets but by manipulating the superstitions and fears of those ashore—simply by blowing the steamer's whistle. The primitive weapons used by both sides in the attack reinforce Marlow's notion that the trip up the river is a trip back in time. Marlow's response to the helmsman's death reflects the general atmosphere of contradiction and absurdity: rather than mourning his right-hand man, Marlow changes his socks and shoes.

In the meantime, tension continues to build as Marlow draws nearer to Kurtz. After the attack, Marlow speculates that Kurtz may be dead, but the strange message and the book full of notes left with the firewood suggest otherwise. Marlow does not need to be told to "hurry up": his eagerness to meet Kurtz draws him onward. To meet Kurtz will be to create a coherent whole in a world sorely lacking in such things; by matching the man with his voice, Marlow hopes to come to an understanding about what happens to men in places like the Congo.

PART II (CONTINUED)

Marlow's digression about Kurtz through his meeting with the Russian trader.

SUMMARY
Marlow breaks into the narrative here to offer a digression on Kurtz. He notes that Kurtz had a fiancée, his Intended (as Kurtz called her), waiting for him in Europe. Marlow attaches no importance to Kurtz's fiancée, since, for him, women exist in an alternate fantasy world. What Marlow does find significant about Kurtz's Intended, though, is the air of possession Kurtz assumed when speaking about her: indeed, Kurtz spoke of everything—ivory, the Inner Station, the river—as being innately his. It is this sense of dark mastery that disturbs Marlow most. Marlow also mentions a report Kurtz has written at the request of the International Society for the Suppression of Savage Customs. The report is eloquent and powerful, if lacking in practical suggestions. It concludes, however, with a handwritten postscript: "Exterminate all the brutes!" Marlow suggests that this coda, the "exposition of [Kurtz's] method," is the result of Kurtz's absorption into native life—that by the time he came to write this note he had assumed a position of power with respect to the natives and had been a participant in "unspeakable rites," where sacrifices had been made in his name. At this point, Marlow also reveals that he feels he is responsible for the "care of [Kurtz's] memory," and that he has no choice but to remember and continue to talk about the man.

At the time Marlow is telling his story, he is still unsure whether Kurtz was worth the lives lost on his behalf; thus, at this point, he returns to his dead helmsman and the journey up the river. Marlow blames the helmsman's death on the man's own lack of restraint: had the helmsman not tried to fire at the men on the riverbank, he would not have been killed. Marlow drags the helmsman's body out of the pilothouse and throws it overboard. The pilgrims are indignant that the man will not receive a proper burial, and the cannibals seem to mourn the loss of a potential meal. The pilgrims have concluded Kurtz must be dead and the Inner Station destroyed, but they are cheered at the crushing defeat they believe they dealt their unseen attackers. Marlow remains skeptical and sarcastically congratulates them on the amount of smoke they have managed to produce. Suddenly, the Inner Station comes into view, somewhat decayed but still standing.

A white man, the Russian trader, beckons to them from the shore. He wears a gaudy patchwork suit and babbles incessantly. He is aware they have been attacked but tells them that everything will now be okay. The manager and the pilgrims go up the hill to retrieve Kurtz, while the Russian boards the ship to converse with Marlow. He tells Marlow that the natives mean no harm (although he is less than convincing on this point), and he confirms Marlow's theory that the ship's whistle is the best means of defense, since it will scare the natives off. He gives a brief account of himself: he has been a merchant seaman and was outfitted by a Dutch trading house to go into the African interior. Marlow gives him the book on seamanship that had been left with the firewood, and the trader is very happy to have it back. As it turns out, what Marlow had thought were encoded notes are simply notes written in Russian. The Russian trader tells Marlow that he has had trouble restraining the natives, and he suggests that the steamer was attacked because the natives do not want Kurtz to leave. The Russian also offers yet another enigmatic picture of Kurtz. According to the trader, one does not talk to Kurtz but listens to him. The trader credits Kurtz for having "enlarged his mind."

ANALYSIS

The interruption and digression at the beginning of this section suggests that Marlow has begun to feel the need to justify his own conduct. Marlow speaks of his fascination with Kurtz as something over which he has no control, as if Kurtz refuses to be forgotten. This is one of a number of instances in which Marlow suggests that a person's responsibility for his actions is not clear-cut. The Russian trader is another example of this: Marlow does not clarify whether the trader follows Kurtz because of Kurtz's charisma, or because of the trader's weakness or insanity.

Marlow repeatedly characterizes Kurtz as a voice, suggesting that eloquence is his defining trait. But Kurtz's eloquence is empty. Moreover, the picture that Marlow paints of Kurtz is extremely ironic. Both in Europe and in Africa, Kurtz is reputed to be a great humanitarian. Whereas the other employees of the

Company only want to make a profit or to advance to a better position within the Company, Kurtz embodies the ideals and fine sentiments with which Europeans justified imperialism—particularly the idea that Europeans brought light and civilization to savage peoples. But when Marlow discovers him, Kurtz has become so ruthless and rapacious that even the other managers are shocked. He refers to the ivory as his own and sets himself up as a primitive god to the natives. He has written a seventeen-page document on the suppression of savage customs, to be disseminated in Europe, but his supposed desire to "civilize" the natives is strikingly contradicted by his postscript, "Exterminate all the brutes!" Marlow is careful to tell his listeners that there was something wrong with Kurtz, some flaw in his character that made him go insane in the isolation of the Inner Station. But the obvious implication of Marlow's story is that the humanitarian ideals and sentiments justifying imperialism are empty, and are merely rationalizations for exploitation and extortion.

Marlow's behavior in the face of an increasingly insane situation demonstrates his refusal to give in to the forces of madness. By throwing the dead helmsman overboard, Marlow spares him from becoming dinner for the cannibals, but he also saves him from what the helmsman might have found even worse: the hypocrisy of a Christian burial by the pilgrims. In contrast with the pilgrims' folly and hypocrisy, Kurtz's serene dictatorship is more attractive to Marlow. In fact, as Marlow's digression at the beginning of this section suggests, right and wrong, sane and insane, are indistinguishable in this world gone mad. Force of personality is the only means by which men are judged. As Marlow's ability to captivate his listeners with his story suggests, charisma may be his link with Kurtz. What the Russian trader says of Kurtz is true of Marlow, too: he is a man to whom people listen, not someone with whom they converse. Thus, the darkness in Kurtz may repel Marlow mostly because it reflects his own internal darkness.

PART III

*The Russian trader's description of Kurtz through the
Russian trader's departure from the Inner Station.*

SUMMARY

The Russian trader begs Marlow to take Kurtz away quickly. He
recounts for Marlow his initial meeting with Kurtz, telling him
that Kurtz and the trader spent a night camped in the forest
together, during which Kurtz discoursed on a broad range of top-
ics. The trader again asserts that listening to Kurtz has greatly
enlarged his mind. His connection to Kurtz, however, has gone
through periods of rise and decline. He nursed Kurtz through
two illnesses but sometimes would not see him for long periods of
time, during which Kurtz was out raiding the countryside for
ivory with a native tribe he had gotten to follow him. Although
Kurtz has behaved erratically and once even threatened to shoot
the trader over a small stash of ivory, the trader nevertheless
insists that Kurtz cannot be judged as one would judge a normal
man. He has tried to get Kurtz to return to civilization several
times. The Russian tells Marlow that Kurtz is extremely ill now.
As he listens to the trader, Marlow idly looks through his binoc-
ulars and sees that what he had originally taken for ornamental
balls on the tops of fence posts in the station compound are actually severed heads turned to face the station house. He is repelled
but not particularly surprised. The Russian apologetically
explains that these are the heads of rebels, an explanation that
makes Marlow laugh out loud. The Russian makes a point of telling Marlow that he has had no medicine or supplies with which
to treat Kurtz; he also asserts that Kurtz has been shamefully
abandoned by the Company.

At that moment, the pilgrims emerge from the station-house with
Kurtz on an improvised stretcher, and a group of natives rushes out
of the forest with a piercing cry. Kurtz speaks to the natives, and the
natives withdraw and allow the party to pass. The manager and the
pilgrims lay Kurtz in one of the ship's cabins and give him his mail,
which they have brought from the Central Station. Someone has
written to Kurtz about Marlow, and Kurtz tells him that he is "glad"
to see him. The manager enters the cabin to speak with Kurtz, and
Marlow withdraws to the steamer's deck. From here he sees two

natives standing near the river with impressive headdresses and spears, and a beautiful native woman draped in ornaments pacing gracefully along the shore. She stops and stares out at the steamer for a while and then moves away into the forest. Marlow notes that she must be wearing several elephant tusks' worth of ornaments. The Russian implies that she is Kurtz's mistress, and states that she has caused him trouble through her influence over Kurtz. He adds that he would have tried to shoot her if she had tried to come aboard. The trader's comments are interrupted by the sound of Kurtz yelling at the manager inside the cabin. Kurtz accuses the men of coming for the ivory rather than to help him, and he threatens the manager for interfering with his plans.

The manager comes out and takes Marlow aside, telling him that they have done everything possible for Kurtz, but that his unsound methods have closed the district off to the Company for the time being. He says he plans on reporting Kurtz's "complete want of judgment" to the Company's directors. Thoroughly disgusted by the manager's hypocritical condemnation of Kurtz, Marlow tells the manager that he thinks Kurtz is a "remarkable man." With this statement, Marlow permanently alienates himself from the manager and the rest of the Company functionaries. Like Kurtz, Marlow is now classified among the "unsound." As the manager walks off, the Russian approaches again, to confide in Marlow that Kurtz ordered the attack on the steamer, hoping that the manager would assume he was dead and turn back. After the Russian asks Marlow to protect Kurtz's reputation, Marlow tells the Russian that the manager has spoken of having the Russian hanged. The trader is not surprised and, after hitting Marlow up for tobacco, gun cartridges, and shoes, leaves in a canoe with some native paddlers.

ANALYSIS

Until this point, Marlow's narrative has featured prominently mysterious signs and symbols, which Marlow has struggled to interpret. Now he confronts the reality of the Inner Station, and witnesses that symbols possess a disturbing power to define "reality" and influence people. The natives perceive Kurtz as a mythical deity and think that the guns carried by his followers are lightning bolts, symbols of power rather than actual weapons. Marlow and the Russian trader are aware of the guns' power to kill, however, and they react nervously at Kurtz's show of force. Kurtz himself acts as a symbol for all of the other characters, not only the natives. To the Russian trader, he is a source of knowledge about everything from economics to love. To Marlow, Kurtz offers "a choice of nightmares," something distinct from the hypocritical evils of the manager. To the manager and the pilgrims, he is a scapegoat, someone they can punish for failing to uphold the "civilized" ideals of colonialism, thereby making themselves seem less reprehensible. The long-awaited appearance of the man himself demonstrates just how empty these formulations are, however. He is little more than a skeleton, and even his name proves not to be an adequate description of him (Kurtz means "short" in German, but Kurtz is tall). Thus, both words and symbols are shown to have little basis in reality.

Kurtz's African mistress provides another example of the power of symbols and the dubious value of words. The woman is never given the title "mistress," although it seems clear that she and Kurtz have a sexual relationship. To acknowledge through the use of the term that a white man and a black woman could be lovers seems to be more than the manager and the Russian trader are willing to do. Despite their desire to discredit Kurtz, the transgression implied by Kurtz's relationship is not something they want to discuss. To Marlow, the woman is above all an aesthetic and economic object. She is "superb" and "magnificent," dripping with the trappings of wealth. As we have seen in earlier sections of Marlow's narrative, he believes that women represent the ideals of a civilization: it is on their behalf that men undertake economic enterprises, and it is their beauty that comes to symbolize nations and ways of life. Thus, Kurtz's African mistress plays a role strikingly like that of Kurtz's fiancée: like his fiancée, Kurtz's mistress is lavished with material goods, both to keep her in her place and to display his success and wealth.

Marlow and the Russian trader offer alternate perspectives throughout this section. The Russian is naive to the point of idiocy, yet he has much in common with Marlow. Both have come to Africa in search of something experiential, and both end up aligning themselves with Kurtz against other Europeans. The Russian, who seems to exist upon "glamour" and youth, is drawn to the systematic qualities of Kurtz's thought. Although Kurtz behaves irrationally toward him, for the trader, the great man's philosophical mind offers a bulwark against the even greater irrationality of Africa. For Marlow, on the other hand, Kurtz represents the choice of outright perversion over hypocritical justifications of cruelty. Marlow and the Russian are disturbingly similar to one another, as the transfer of responsibility for Kurtz's "reputation" from the Russian to Marlow suggests. The manager's implicit condemnation of Marlow as "unsound" is correct, if for the wrong reasons: by choosing Kurtz, Marlow has, in fact, like the cheerfully idiotic Russian, merely chosen one kind of nightmare over another.

PART III (CONTINUED)

Marlow's nighttime pursuit of Kurtz through the steamship's departure from the Inner Station.

SUMMARY

Remembering the Russian trader's warning, Marlow gets up in the middle of the night and goes out to look around for any sign of trouble. From the deck of the steamer, he sees one of the pilgrims with a group of the cannibals keeping guard over the ivory, and he sees the fires of the natives' camp in the forest. He hears a drum and a steady chanting, which lulls him into a brief sleep. A sudden outburst of yells wakes him, but the loud noise immediately subsides into a rhythmic chanting once again. Marlow glances into Kurtz's cabin only to find that Kurtz is gone. He is unnerved, but he does not raise an alarm, and instead decides to leave the ship to search for Kurtz himself.

He finds a trail in the grass and realizes that Kurtz must be crawling on all fours. Marlow runs along the trail after him; Kurtz hears him coming and rises to his feet. They are now close to the fires of the native camp, and Marlow realizes the danger of his situation, as Kurtz could easily call out to the natives and have him killed. Kurtz tells him to go away and hide, and Marlow looks over and sees the imposing figure of a native sorcerer silhouetted against the fire. Marlow asks Kurtz if he knows what he is doing, and Kurtz replies emphatically that he does. Despite his physical advantage over the invalid, Marlow feels impotent, and threatens to strangle Kurtz if he should call out to the natives. Kurtz bemoans the failure of his grand schemes, and Marlow reassures him that he is thought a success in Europe. Sensing the other man's vulnerability, Marlow tells Kurtz he will be lost if he continues on. Kurtz's resolution falters, and Marlow helps him back to the ship.

The steamer departs the next day at noon, and the natives appear on the shore to watch it go. Three men painted with red earth and wearing horned headdresses wave charms and shout incantations at the ship as it steams away. Marlow places Kurtz in the pilothouse to get some air, and Kurtz watches through the open window as his mistress rushes down to the shore and calls out to him. The crowd responds to her cry with an uproar of its own. Marlow sounds the whistle as he sees the pilgrims get out their rifles, and the crowd scatters, to the pilgrims' dismay. Only the woman remains standing on the shore as the pilgrims open fire, and Marlow's view is obscured by smoke.

ANALYSIS

Marlow describes his developing relationship with Kurtz in terms of intimacy and betrayal. The extravagant symbolism of the previous section is largely absent here. Instead, Marlow and Kurtz confront one another in a dark forest, with no one else around. Marlow seems to stand both physically and metaphorically between Kurtz and a final plunge into madness and depravity, as symbolized by the native sorcerer presiding over the fire at the native camp. It occurs to Marlow that, from a practical standpoint, he should strangle Kurtz. The nearness of the natives puts Marlow in danger, and Kurtz is going to die soon anyway. Yet to kill Kurtz would not only be hypocritical but, for Marlow, impossible. As Marlow perceives it, Kurtz's "crime" is that he has rejected all of the principles and obligations that make up European society. Marlow "could not appeal [to him] in the name of anything high or low." Kurtz has become an entirely self-sufficient unit, a man who has "kicked himself loose of the earth." In a way, the Russian trader is right to claim that Kurtz cannot be judged by normal standards. Kurtz has already judged, and rejected, the standards by which other people are judged, and thus it seems irrelevant to bring such standards back to bear on him.

Marlow suggests that Africa is responsible for Kurtz's current condition. Having rejected European society, Kurtz has been forced to look into his own soul, and this introspection has driven him mad. Kurtz's illness, resulting from his body's inability to function outside of a normal (i.e., European) environment, reflects his psyche's inability to function outside of a normal social environment. Despite the hypocrisy latent in social norms, these norms provide a framework of security and defined expectations within which an individual can exist. In Freudian terms, we might say that Kurtz has lost his superego, and that it is the terror of limitless freedom, with no oversight or punishment, that leads to his madness. Kurtz now knows himself to be capable of anything. Marlow claims that his recognition of this capacity forces him to look into Kurtz's soul, and that his coming face-to-face with Kurtz is his "punishment." Marlow's epiphany about the roots of Kurtz's madness does lead to a moment of profound intimacy between the two men, as Marlow both comes to understand Kurtz's deepest self-awareness and in turn is forced to apply this realization to himself, as he sees that Kurtz's actual depravity mirrors his own potential depravity. Given this, for Marlow to betray Kurtz—whether by killing him or by siding with the manager against him—would be to betray himself. Later in the narrative, when Marlow speaks of his "choice of nightmares," the alternatives of which he speaks are social injustice and cruelty on the one hand, and the realization that one's soul is empty and infinitely capable of depravity on the other hand.

The pilgrims' fervent desire to use the natives for target practice as the steamer departs clearly reflects the former choice. Kurtz's mistress and, more generally, his level of control over the natives at the station are reminders that the kind of self-immolation that Kurtz has chosen has nothing inherently noble about it. Kurtz's realization of his potential for depravity has not kept him from exercising it. Significantly, Kurtz's mistress demonstrates that although Kurtz has "kicked himself loose from the earth," he cannot help but reenact some of the social practices he has rejected. There is something sentimental about her behavior, despite her hard-edged appearance, and her relationship with Kurtz seems to have some of the same characteristics of romance, manipulation, and adoration as a traditional European male-female coupling. Moreover, as was noted in the previous section, with all her finery she has come to symbolize value and economic enterprise, much as a European woman would. Critics have often read her as a racist and misogynist stereotype, and in many ways this is true. However, the fact that Kurtz and Marlow both view her as a symbol rather than as a person is part of the point: we are supposed to recognize that she is actively stereotyped by Kurtz and by Marlow.

PART III (CONTINUED)

Marlow's journey back down the river through his falling ill.

SUMMARY

The current speeds the steamer's progress back toward civilization. The manager, certain that Kurtz will soon be dead, is pleased to have things in hand; he condescendingly ignores Marlow, who is now clearly of the "unsound" but harmless party. The pilgrims are disdainful, and Marlow, for the most part, is left alone with Kurtz. As he had done with the Russian trader, Kurtz takes advantage of his captive audience to hold forth on a variety of subjects. Marlow is alternately impressed and disappointed. Kurtz's philosophical musings are interspersed with grandiose and childish plans for fame and fortune.

> *The brown current ran swiftly out of the heart of darkness, bearing us down towards the sea with twice the speed of our upward progress; and Kurtz's life was running swiftly, too . . .*
>
> *(See QUOTATIONS, p. 52)*

The steamer breaks down, and repairs take some time. Marlow is slowly becoming ill, and the work is hard on him. Kurtz seems troubled, probably because the delay has made him realize that he probably will not make it back to Europe alive. Worried that the manager will gain control of his "legacy," Kurtz gives Marlow a bundle of papers for safekeeping. Kurtz's ramblings become more abstract and more rhetorical as his condition worsens. Marlow believes he is reciting portions of articles he has written for the newspapers: Kurtz thinks it his "duty" to disseminate his ideas. Finally, one night, Kurtz admits to Marlow that he is "waiting for death." As Marlow approaches, Kurtz seems to be receiving some profound knowledge or vision, and the look on his face forces Marlow to stop and stare. Kurtz cries out—"The horror! The horror!"—and Marlow flees, not wanting to watch the man die. He joins the manager in the dining hall, which is suddenly overrun by flies. A moment later, a servant comes in to tell them, "Mistah Kurtz—he dead."

The pilgrims bury Kurtz the next day. Marlow succumbs to illness and nearly dies himself. He suffers greatly, but the worst thing about his near-death experience is his realization that in the end he would have "nothing to say." Kurtz, he realizes, was remarkable because he "had something to say. He said it." Marlow remembers little about the time of his illness. Once he has recovered sufficiently, he leaves Africa and returns to Brussels.

ANALYSIS

Both Kurtz and Marlow experience a brief interlude during which they float between life and death, although their final fates differ. For Kurtz, the imminence of death ironically causes him to seek to return to the world from which he had "kicked himself loose." Suddenly, his legacy and his ideas seem very important to him, and he turns to Marlow to preserve them. Kurtz's final ambitions—to be famous and feted by kings, to have his words read by millions—suggest a desire to change the world. This is a change from his previous formulations, which posited a choice between acquiescence to existing norms or total isolation from society. However, these final schemes of Kurtz's (which Marlow describes as "childish") reflect Kurtz's desire for self-aggrandizement rather than any progressive social program. Kurtz dies. His last words are paradoxically full of meaning yet totally empty. It is possible to read them as an acknowledgment of Kurtz's own misguided life and despicable acts, as a description of his inner darkness; certainly, to do so is not inappropriate. However, it is important to note both their eloquence and their vagueness. True to form, Kurtz dies in a spasm of eloquence. His last words are poetic and profound, delivered in his remarkable voice. However, they are so nonspecific that they defy interpretation. The best one can do is to guess at their meaning.

> *I was within a hair's-breadth of the last opportunity for pronouncement, and I found with humiliation that probably I would have nothing to say.*
>
> *(See* QUOTATIONS, *p. 53)*

Does this mean that Marlow is wrong, that Kurtz has "nothing," not "something to say"? Kurtz's last words could refer to the terrible nothingness at the heart of his soul and his ideas, the ultimate failure of his "destiny." In a way this is true: Kurtz's agony seems to be a response to a generalized lack of substance. In his dying words as in his life, though, Kurtz creates an enigma, an object for contemplation, which certainly is something. His legacy, in fact, would seem to be Marlow, who, like the Russian trader, seems to have had his mind "enlarged" by Kurtz. Marlow, though, finds that he himself has "nothing" to say, and thus Kurtz's life and his dying words oscillate between absolute emptiness and an overabundance of meaning. The "horror" is either nothing or everything, but it is not simply "something."

The actual moment of Kurtz's death is narrated indirectly. First, Kurtz's words—"The horror! The horror!"—anticipate and mark its beginning. Then flies, the symbol of slow, mundane decay and disintegration (as opposed to catastrophic or dramatic destruction), swarm throughout the ship, as if to mark the actual moment. Finally, the servant arrives to bring the moment to its close with his surly, unpoetic words. The roughness of "Mistah Kurtz—he dead" contrasts with Kurtz's self-generated epitaph, again bringing a blunt reality (death) into conflict with a subjective state (horror). It is interesting to consider why T. S. Eliot might have chosen the servant's line as the epigraph to his poem "The Hollow Men." The impenetrability of the brief moment of Kurtz's death and his reduction to something "buried in a muddy hole" indicate the final impossibility of describing either Kurtz or his ideas.

Kurtz's death is very nearly followed by Marlow's demise. Although both men's illnesses are blamed on climate, it seems as if they are both also the result of existential crisis. Furthermore, an element of metaphorical contagion seems to be involved, as Kurtz transmits both his memory and his poor health to Marlow. Unlike Kurtz, though, Marlow recovers. Having "nothing to say" seems to save him. He does not slip into the deadly paradox of wanting to be both free of society and an influence on it, and he will not have to sacrifice himself for his ideas. For Marlow, guarding Kurtz's legacy is not inconsistent with isolation from society. Remaining loyal to Kurtz is best done by remaining true to his experience, and by not offering up his story to those who will misinterpret or fail to understand it. Marlow keeps these principles in mind once he arrives in Brussels. His reasons for telling this story to his audience aboard the *Nellie* are more difficult to discern.

PART III (CONTINUED)

Marlow's return to Brussels through the conclusion.

SUMMARY

Marlow barely survives his illness. Eventually he returns to the "sepulchral city," Brussels. He resents the people there for their petty self-importance and smug complacency. His aunt nurses him back to health, but his disorder is more emotional than physical. A bespectacled representative of the Company comes to retrieve the packet of papers Kurtz entrusted to Marlow, but Marlow will give him only the pamphlet on the "Suppression of Savage Customs," with the postscript (the handwritten "Exterminate all the brutes!") torn off. The man threatens legal action to obtain the rest of the packet's contents. Another man, calling himself Kurtz's cousin, appears and takes some letters to the family. The cousin tells him that Kurtz had been a great musician, although he does not elaborate further. Marlow and the cousin ponder Kurtz's myriad talents and decide that he is best described as a "universal genius." A journalist colleague of Kurtz's appears and takes the pamphlet for publication. This man believes Kurtz's true skills were in popular or extremist politics.

Finally, Marlow is left with only a few letters and a picture of Kurtz's Intended. Marlow goes to see her without really knowing why. Kurtz's memory comes flooding back to him as he stands on her doorstep. He finds the Intended still in mourning, though it has been over a year since Kurtz's death. He gives her the packet, and she asks if he knew Kurtz well. He replies that he knew him as well as it is possible for one man to know another.

His presence fulfills her need for a sympathetic ear, and she continually praises Kurtz. Her sentimentality begins to anger Marlow, but he holds back his annoyance until it gives way to pity. She says she will mourn Kurtz forever, and asks Marlow to repeat his last words to give her something upon which to sustain herself. Marlow lies and tells her that Kurtz's last word was her name. She responds that she was certain that this was the case. Marlow ends his story here, and the narrator looks off into the dark sky, which makes the waterway seem "to lead into the heart of an immense darkness."

ANALYSIS

Marlow's series of encounters with persons from Kurtz's former life makes him question the value he places on his memories of Kurtz. Kurtz's cousin and the journalist both offer a version of Kurtz that seems not to resemble the man Marlow knew. Kurtz, in fact, seems to have been all things to all people—someone who has changed their life and now serves as a kind of symbolic figure presiding over their existence. This makes Marlow's own experience of Kurtz less unique and thus perhaps less meaningful. The fact that he shares Kurtz with all of these overconfident, self-important people, most of whom will never leave Brussels, causes Kurtz to seem common, and less profound. In reality, Marlow's stream of visitors do not raise any new issues: in their excessive praise of Kurtz and their own lack of perspective, they resemble the Russian trader, who also took Kurtz as a kind of guru.

Marlow goes to see Kurtz's Intended in a state of profound uncertainty. He is unsure whether his version of Kurtz has any value either as a reflection of reality or as a philosophical construct. In response to the woman's simple question as to whether he knew Kurtz well, he can only reply that he knew him "'as well as it is possible for one man to know another.'" Given what the preceding narrative has shown about the possibilities for "knowing" another person in any meaningful sense, the reader can easily see that Marlow's reply to Kurtz's Intended is a qualification, not an affirmation: Marlow barely knows himself. By the end of Marlow's visit with the woman, the reader is also aware, even if Marlow is not, that the kinds of illusions and untruths which Marlow accuses women of perpetuating are in fact not dissimilar from those fictions men use to understand their own experiences and justify such things as colonialism. Marlow has much more in common with Kurtz's Intended than he would like to admit.

Kurtz's Intended, like Marlow's aunt and Kurtz's mistress, is a problematic female figure. Marlow praises her for her "mature capacity for fidelity, for belief, for suffering," suggesting that the most valuable traits in a woman are passive. Conrad's portrayal of the Intended has thus been criticized for having misogynist overtones, and there is some justification for this point of view. She is a repository of conservative ideas about what it means to be white and European, upholding fine-sounding but ultimately useless notions of heroism and romance.

Although both Marlow and the Intended construct idealized versions of Kurtz to make sense out of their respective worlds, in the end, Marlow's version of Kurtz is upheld as the more profound one. Marlow emphasizes his disgust at the complacency of the people he meets in Brussels in order to validate his own store of worldly experience. Marlow's narrative implies that his version of Kurtz, as well as his accounts of Africa and imperialism, are inherently better and truer than other people's because of what he has experienced. This notion is based on traditional ideas of heroism, involving quests and trials in the pursuit of knowledge. In fact, by seeming to legitimize activities like imperialism for their experiential value for white men—in other words, by making it appear that Africa is the key to philosophical truth—the ending of *Heart of Darkness* introduces a much greater horror than any Marlow has encountered in the Congo. Are the evils of colonialism excusable in the name of "truth" or knowledge, even if they are not justifiable in the name of wealth? This paradox accounts at least partially for the novella's frame story. Marlow recounts his experiences to his friends because doing so establishes an implicit comparison. The other men aboard the *Nellie* are the kind of men who benefit economically from imperialism, while Marlow has benefited mainly experientially. While Marlow's "truth" may be more profound than that of his friends or Kurtz's Intended, it may not justify the cost of its own acquisition.

IMPORTANT QUOTATIONS EXPLAINED

1. *"The word 'ivory' rang in the air, was whispered, was sighed. You would think they were praying to it. A taint of imbecile rapacity blew through it all, like a whiff from some corpse. By Jove! I've never seen anything so unreal in my life. And outside, the silent wilderness surrounding this cleared speck on the earth struck me as something great and invincible, like evil or truth, waiting patiently for the passing away of this fantastic invasion."*

This quote, from the fourth section of Part I, offers Marlow's initial impression of the Central Station. The word "ivory" has taken on a life of its own for the men who work for the Company. To them, it is far more than the tusk of an elephant; it represents economic freedom, social advancement, an escape from a life of being an employee. The word has lost all connection to any physical reality and has itself become an object of worship. Marlow's reference to a decaying corpse is both literal and figurative: elephants and native Africans both die as a result of the white man's pursuit of ivory, and the entire enterprise is rotten at the core. The cruelties and the greed are both part of a greater, timeless evil, yet they are petty in the scheme of the greater order of the natural world.

2.   *"In a few days the Eldorado Expedition went into the patient wilderness, that closed upon it as the sea closes over a diver. Long afterwards the news came that all the donkeys were dead. I know nothing as to the fate of the less valuable animals. They, no doubt, like the rest of us, found what they deserved. I did not inquire."*

During the first section of Part II, Marlow watches the Eldorado Exploring Expedition, a band of freelance bandits, reequip and then depart from the Central Station. This enigmatic report is the only news he receives concerning their fate. The dry irony of this quote is characteristic of Marlow, who by this point has truly come to see white men as the "less valuable animals." Although he chalks up the Expedition's fate to some idea of destiny or just reward, Marlow has already come to distrust such moral formulations: this is why he does not seek further information about the Expedition. Again he mentions a "patient wilderness": the Expedition's fate is insignificant in the face of larger catastrophes and even less meaningful when considered in the scope of nature's time frame.

3. "It was unearthly, and the men were—No, they were not inhuman. Well, you know, that was the worst of it—the suspicion of their not being inhuman. It would come slowly to one. They howled and leaped, and spun, and made horrid faces; but what thrilled you was just the thought of their humanity—like yours—the thought of your remote kinship with this wild and passionate uproar. Ugly. Yes, it was ugly enough; but if you were man enough you would admit to yourself that there was in you just the faintest trace of a response to the terrible frankness of that noise, a dim suspicion of there being a meaning in it which you—you so remote from the night of first ages—could comprehend. And why not?"

As Marlow journeys up the river toward the Inner Station in the first section of Part II, he catches occasional glimpses of native villages along the riverbanks. More often, though, he simply hears things: drums, chants, howls. These engage his imagination, and the fact that they do so troubles him, because it suggests, as he says, a "kinship" with these men, whom he has so far been able to classify as "inhuman." This moment is one of several in the text in which Marlow seems to admit the limits of his own perception. These moments allow for a reading of Heart of Darkness that is much more critical of colonialism and much more ironic about the stereotypes it engenders. Nevertheless, it is important to notice that Marlow still casts Africans as a primitive version of himself rather than as potential equals.

QUOTATIONS

4. *"The brown current ran swiftly out of the heart of darkness, bearing us down towards the sea with twice the speed of our upward progress; and Kurtz's life was running swiftly, too, ebbing, ebbing out of his heart into the sea of inexorable time. . . . I saw the time approaching when I would be left alone of the party of 'unsound method.'"*

This quote, which comes as the steamer begins its voyage back from the Inner Station in the third section of Part III, with Kurtz and his ivory aboard, brings together the images of the river and the "heart of darkness" which it penetrates. The river is something that separates Marlow from the African interior: while on the river he is exterior to, even if completely surrounded by, the jungle. Furthermore, despite its "brown current," the river inexorably brings him back to white civilization. The first sentence of this quote suggests that Marlow and Kurtz have been able to leave the "heart of darkness" behind, but Kurtz's life seems to be receding along with the "darkness," and Marlow, too, has been permanently scarred by it, since he is now ineradicably marked as being of Kurtz's party. Thus, it seems that the "darkness" is in fact internalized, that it is part of some fundamental if ironic "unsoundness."

5. *"I was within a hair's-breadth of the last opportunity for pronouncement, and I found with humiliation that probably I would have nothing to say. This is the reason why I affirm that Kurtz was a remarkable man. He had something to say. He said it. . . . He had summed up—he had judged. 'The horror!' He was a remarkable man."*

At the beginning of the final section of Part III, Marlow has just recovered from his near-fatal illness. His "nothing to say" is not reflective of a lack of substance but rather of his realization that anything he might have to say would be so ambiguous and so profound as to be impossible to put into words. Kurtz, on the other hand, is "remarkable" for his ability to cut through ambiguity, to create a definite "something." Paradoxically, though, the final formulation of that "something" is so vague as to approach "nothing": " 'The horror!' " could be almost anything. However, perhaps Kurtz is most fascinating to Marlow because he has had the courage to judge, to deny ambiguity. Marlow is aware of Kurtz's intelligence and the man's appreciation of paradox, so he also knows that Kurtz's rabid systematization of the world around him has been an act and a lie. Yet Kurtz, on the strength of his hubris and his charisma, has created out of himself a way of organizing the world that contradicts generally accepted social models. Most important, he has created an impressive legacy: Marlow will ponder Kurtz's words (" 'The horror!' ") and Kurtz's memory for the rest of his life. By turning himself into an enigma, Kurtz has done the ultimate: he has ensured his own immortality.

QUOTATIONS

KEY FACTS

FULL TITLE
Heart of Darkness

AUTHOR
Joseph Conrad

TYPE OF WORK
Novella (between a novel and a short story in length and scope)

GENRE
Symbolism, colonial literature, adventure tale, frame story, almost a romance in its insistence on heroism and the supernatural and its preference for the symbolic over the realistic

LANGUAGE
English

TIME AND PLACE WRITTEN
England, 1898–1899; inspired by Conrad's journey to the Congo in 1890

DATE OF FIRST PUBLICATION
Serialized in *Blackwood's Magazine* in 1899; published in 1902 in the volume *Youth: A Narrative; and Two Other Stories*

PUBLISHER
J. M. Dent & Sons, Ltd.

NARRATOR
There are two narrators: an anonymous passenger on a pleasure ship, who listens to Marlow's story, and Marlow himself, a middle-aged ship's captain

POINT OF VIEW
The first narrator speaks in the first-person plural, on behalf of four other passengers who listen to Marlow's tale. Marlow narrates his story in the first person, describing only what he witnessed and experienced, and providing his own commentary on the story.

TONE
  Ambivalent: Marlow is disgusted at the brutality of the
  Company and horrified by Kurtz's degeneration, but he claims
  that any thinking man would be tempted into similar behavior.

TENSE
  Past

SETTING (TIME)
  Latter part of the nineteenth century, probably sometime
  between 1876 and 1892

SETTING (PLACE)
  Opens on the Thames River outside London, where Marlow is
  telling the story that makes up Heart of Darkness. Events of the
  story take place in Brussels, at the Company's offices, and in the
  Congo, then a Belgian territory.

PROTAGONIST
  Marlow

MAJOR CONFLICT
  Both Marlow and Kurtz confront a conflict between their images
  of themselves as "civilized" Europeans and the temptation to
  abandon morality completely once they leave the context of
  European society.

RISING ACTION
  The brutality Marlow witnesses in the Company's employees,
  the rumors he hears that Kurtz is a remarkable and humane man,
  and the numerous examples of Europeans breaking down
  mentally or physically in the environment of Africa.

CLIMAX
  Marlow's discovery, upon reaching the Inner Station, that Kurtz
  has completely abandoned European morals and norms of
  behavior

FALLING ACTION
  Marlow's acceptance of responsibility for Kurtz's legacy,
  Marlow's encounters with Company officials and Kurtz's family
  and friends, Marlow's visit to Kurtz's Intended

THEMES

The hypocrisy of imperialism, madness as a result of imperialism, the absurdity of evil

MOTIFS

Darkness (very seldom opposed by light), interiors vs. surfaces (kernel/shell, coast/inland, station/forest, etc.), ironic understatement, hyperbolic language, inability to find words to describe situation adequately, images of ridiculous waste, upriver vs. downriver/toward and away from Kurtz/away from and back toward civilization (quest or journey structure)

SYMBOLS

Rivers, fog, women (Kurtz's Intended, his African mistress), French warship shelling forested coast, grove of death, severed heads on fence posts, Kurtz's "Report," dead helmsman, maps, "whited sepulchre" of Brussels, knitting women in Company offices, man trying to fill bucket with hole in it

FORESHADOWING

Permeates every moment of the narrative—mostly operates on the level of imagery, which is consistently dark, gloomy, and threatening

STUDY QUESTIONS & ESSAY TOPICS

STUDY QUESTIONS

1. *The Nigerian writer Chinua Achebe has claimed that* HEART OF DARKNESS *is an "offensive and deplorable book" that "set[s] Africa up as a foil to Europe, as a place of negations at once remote and vaguely familiar, in comparison with which Europe's own state of spiritual grace will be manifest." Achebe says that Conrad does not provide enough of an outside frame of reference to enable the novel to be read as ironic or critical of imperialism. Based on the evidence in the text, argue for or against Achebe's assertion.*

This novel opens with Marlow noting that England was once one of the dark places of the earth. This can be read two ways. First, Marlow may mean that "Western" civilization is just as barbarous as African civilizations. This reading may contradict the European belief that white men are more "civilized" than their colonial subjects, but it hardly mitigates racist notions about primitive or degraded "savages": it just means that Europeans are as "bad" as that which they have constructed as the lowest form of humanity. The second way to read Marlow's comment is as a reference to the historical precedent for colonization of other peoples. England, after all, was once a Roman colony. Again, this reading is more ambiguous than it seems. On the one hand, it implies that all peoples need a more advanced civilization to come along and save them; on the other hand, though, it also implies that the British would and did react to an exploitative colonial presence in the same way the Africans are reacting. The ambiguity and angst inherent in the statements this book makes about imperialism suggest that Achebe's condemnation is too simple. Additionally, moments of irony and narrative unreliability are scattered throughout the text, suggesting that Conrad does indeed provide a framework against which Heart of Darkness can be read as critical or ironic. At the same time, the fact that Africa is set up as a place where white men can go to have profound experiences and think philosophically could be read as reinforcing Achebe's claim that "Africa [is used] as [a] setting and backdrop which eliminates the African as human factor" in a troubling way.

2. *Discuss the importance of the Congo River in this narrative. Why does Marlow travel primarily by boat and seldom on land?*

The river is a space that allows Marlow to be simultaneously within and removed from the African interior. On the river he is isolated, a spectator. To discern his surroundings, he must watch and interpret the thin margin of land at the river's edge: from this he must guess at what lies behind and all around him. This inability to penetrate the continent's interior is a symptom of the larger problem with interiors and exteriors in the book. Marlow is unable to see into the interior selves of those around him; instead, he, like the doctor he visits before he departs for Africa, must base his knowledge on exterior signs. At the beginning of *Heart of Darkness,* the unnamed narrator discusses the fact that for Marlow the meaning of a story or an episode lies in its exterior rather than in any kernel of meaning at its heart. Throughout the book Marlow is indeed confronted with a series of exteriors, of which travel on the river is a prominent example. The caravan that goes from the Outer Station to the Central Station provides Marlow with his only opportunity for travel inland, and he finds there only a depopulated waste scattered with a few corpses: it tells him nothing. At the very least, travel by river lays before Marlow a surface to interpret.

3.   *Marlow constantly uses vague and often redundant*
      phrases like "unspeakable secrets" and "inconceivable
      mystery." At other times, however, he is capable of
      powerful imagery and considerable eloquence. Why
      does Marlow use vague and "inconclusive" language so
      frequently?

In its treatment of imperialism and individual experience, *Heart of Darkness* is on many levels a story about ambiguity. Thus, Marlow's use of language is at the very least thematic. Throughout the book, words assume a bizarre, almost fetishistic power: "ivory," for example, becomes almost more concrete than the elephant tusks themselves. The name "Kurtz" also takes on a life of its own, as it comes to stand for a set of legends and rumors rather than an actual man. Marlow becomes suspicious of words, as they threaten to overtake and distort the meaning they are supposed to convey. On the one hand, words fail to reflect reality adequately, and reality is often so paradoxical that the words don't exist to describe it; but, on the other hand, words sometimes take on an independent life of their own. Marlow's vague terminology, in addition to possessing a lyrical beauty, helps him to negotiate the dual threats of language.

Suggested Essay Topics

1. Why does HEART OF DARKNESS have two competing heroes? Make the case for either Marlow or Kurtz as the true "hero" of the book.

2. Discuss the framing story that structures HEART OF DARKNESS. Why is it important to narrate Marlow in the act of telling his story?

3. Interpret Kurtz's dying words ("The horror! The horror!"). What do they mean? What are the possible "horrors" to which he is referring? Why is Marlow the recipient of Kurtz's last words?

4. Contrast Kurtz's African mistress with his Intended. Are both negative portrayals of women? Describe how each functions in the narrative. Does it make any difference in your interpretation to know that Conrad supported the women's suffrage movement?

5. Describe the use of "darkness" both in the book's title and as a symbol throughout the text. What does darkness represent? Is its meaning constant or does it change?

6. How does physical illness relate to madness? How does one's environment relate to one's mental state in this book?

7. Why does Marlow lie to Kurtz's fiancée about Kurtz's last words? Why not tell her the truth, or tell her that Kurtz had no last words, rather than affirming her sentimental and mundane ideas?

REVIEW & RESOURCES

QUIZ

1. *Heart of Darkness* opens in what setting?

   A. A boat on the Congo River
   B. A boat on the Thames River
   C. The Company's offices in Brussels
   D. The Outer Station

2. Where does Kurtz die?

   A. At the Inner Station
   B. In Brussels
   C. Aboard Marlow's steamer
   D. In the jungle

3. What does Marlow discover atop the fence posts at the Inner Station?

   A. Human heads
   B. Monkey skulls
   C. Dead infants
   D. The Company flag

4. The Company trades primarily in

   A. Gold
   B. Slaves
   C. Bananas
   D. Ivory

5. Which of the following receives Kurtz's "Report" after his death?

   A. Marlow's aunt
   B. Kurtz's "Intended"
   C. A representative of the Company
   D. A journalist

6.   Most of Marlow's adventures take place in

   A.   Kenya
   B.   Rhodesia
   C.   The Congo
   D.   England

7.   Which of the following is not something that Marlow gives to the Russian trader?

   A.   Food
   B.   Gun cartridges
   C.   Tobacco
   D.   Shoes

8.   What do the men at the Central Station hear about the fate of the Eldorado Exploring Expedition?

   A.   That they have been successful and are returning with lots of ivory
   B.   That the expedition's pack animals are dead
   C.   That the men have been ambushed and killed by natives
   D.   That the expedition has found Kurtz

9.   At the end of his "Report" on the natives, Kurtz writes:

   A.   "Exterminate all the brutes!"
   B.   "God help us!"
   C.   "No more death!"
   D.   "God save the King!"

10.   What one thing does Marlow need to repair his wrecked steamer?

   A.   Steel plates
   B.   A new boiler
   C.   Tools
   D.   Rivets

11. Which of the following does not accompany Marlow on his journey up the river from the Central Station?

   A. The chief accountant
   B. The general manager
   C. The cannibals
   D. The pilgrims

12. How does Marlow's helmsman die?

   A. He is killed and eaten by the cannibals
   B. He is shot by an angry pilgrim
   C. He is impaled on a spear thrown from the riverbank
   D. He falls overboard and drowns

13. The Company is

   A. English
   B. French
   C. Dutch
   D. Belgian

14. At the Company's offices Marlow encounters

   A. Kurtz
   B. Kurtz's fiancée
   C. Two old women knitting
   D. A Russian trader

15. Why are the cannibals aboard the steamer hungry?

   A. The pilgrims threw their rotting meat overboard
   B. There are no humans for them to eat
   C. They have no way to make a fire to cook their food
   D. They are fasting for religious reasons

16. Who is ultimately responsible for the attack on the steamer?

   A. The Russian trader
   B. The general manager
   C. Kurtz
   D. Marlow

17. Marlow's predecessor with the Company dies as a result of a quarrel over

    A. Ivory
    B. Hens
    C. A card game
    D. A woman

18. The last person Marlow sees in Brussels is

    A. The president of the Company
    B. His aunt
    C. Kurtz's cousin
    D. Kurtz's fiancée

19. Who helps Marlow to get a job with the Company?

    A. Kurtz
    B. The Director of Companies
    C. His father
    D. His aunt

20. What does the Russian trader leave downriver for the approaching steamer?

    A. Firewood
    B. Water
    C. A map
    D. Food

21. Before he goes to Africa, Marlow has been on a voyage through

    A. The South Pacific
    B. Asia
    C. Central America
    D. Alaska

22. Where does Marlow encounter the "grove of death"?

    A. Brussels
    B. The Outer Station
    C. The Central Station
    D. The Inner Station

23. The chief accountant's most notable characteristic is

    A. His bald head
    B. His spotless white clothing
    C. His shining black shoes
    D. His unusual hat

24. At the Central Station the native laborers burn

    A. A hut full of trade goods
    B. Marlow's steamer
    C. The chief accountant's quarters
    D. The surrounding forest

25. What are Kurtz's last words?

    A. "Exterminate all the brutes!"
    B. "The horror! The horror!"
    C. His fiancée's name
    D. "God help me!"

ANSWER KEY:
1: B; 2: C; 3: A; 4: D; 5: D; 6: C; 7: A; 8: B; 9: A; 10: D; 11:
A; 12: C; 13: D; 14: C; 15: A; 16: A; 17: B; 18: D; 19: D; 20:
A; 21: B; 22: B; 23: B; 24: A; 25: B

SUGGESTIONS FOR FURTHER READING

ACHEBE, CHINUA. " 'An Image of Africa': Racism in Conrad's 'HEART OF DARKNESS.' " In HEART OF DARKNESS: *An Authoritative Text, Backgrounds and Sources, Criticism,* ed. Robert Kimbrough. New York: Norton, 1988.

BLOOM, HAROLD, ed. *Marlow.* New York: Chelsea House Publishers, 1992.

CHENG, YUAN-JUNG. *Heralds of the Postmodern: Madness and Fiction in Conrad, Woolf, and Lessing.* New York: Peter Lang, 1999.

CONRAD, JOSEPH. HEART OF DARKNESS. New York: W. W. Norton & Co., 1963.

EAGLETON, TERRY. *Criticism and Ideology: A Study in Marxist Literary Theory.* London: Verso, 1976.

FIRCHOW, PETER EDGERLY. *Envisioning Africa: Racism and Imperialism in Conrad's* HEART OF DARKNESS. Lexington: University of Kentucky Press, 2000.

GUETTI, JAMES L. *The Limits of Metaphor: A Study of Melville, Conrad, and Faulkner.* Ithaca, New York: Cornell University Press, 1967.

NAVARETTE, SUSAN J. *The Shape of Fear: Horror and the Fin-de-Siecle Culture of Decadence.* Lexington: University of Kentucky Press, 1998.

STAPE, J. H., ed. *The Cambridge Companion to Joseph Conrad.* Cambridge: Cambridge University Press, 1996.

SPARKNOTES
TEST PREPARATION
GUIDES

The SparkNotes team figured it was time to cut standardized tests down to size. We've studied the tests for you, so that SparkNotes test prep guides are:

Smarter
Packed with critical-thinking skills and test-
taking strategies that will improve your score.

Better
Fully up to date, covering all new features of the tests,
with study tips on every type of question.

Faster
Our books cover exactly what you need to
know for the test. No more, no less.

SparkNotes™ Literature Guides

1984

The Adventures of
  Huckleberry Finn

The Adventures of Tom
  Sawyer

The Aeneid

All Quiet on the
  Western Front

And Then There Were
  None

Angela's Ashes

Animal Farm

Anna Karenina

Anne of Green Gables

Anthem

Antony and Cleopatra

Aristotle's Ethics

As I Lay Dying

As You Like It

Atlas Shrugged

The Awakening

The Autobiography of
  Malcolm X

The Bean Trees

The Bell Jar

Beloved

Beowulf

Billy Budd

Black Boy

Bless Me, Ultima

The Bluest Eye

Brave New World

The Brothers
  Karamazov

The Call of the Wild

Candide

The Canterbury Tales

Catch-22

The Catcher in the Rye

The Chocolate War

The Chosen

Cold Mountain

Cold Sassy Tree

The Color Purple

The Count of Monte
  Cristo

Crime and Punishment

The Crucible

Cry, the Beloved
  Country

Cyrano de Bergerac

David Copperfield

Death of a Salesman

The Death of Socrates

The Diary of a Young
  Girl

A Doll's House

Don Quixote

Dr. Faustus

Dr. Jekyll and Mr. Hyde

Dracula

Dune

East of Eden

Edith Hamilton's
  Mythology

Emma

Ethan Frome

Fahrenheit 451

Fallen Angels

A Farewell to Arms

Farewell to Manzanar

Flowers for Algernon

For Whom the Bell
  Tolls

The Fountainhead

Frankenstein

The Giver

The Glass Menagerie

Gone With the Wind

The Good Earth

The Grapes of Wrath

Great Expectations

The Great Gatsby

Greek Classics

Grendel

Gulliver's Travels

Hamlet

The Handmaid's Tale

Hard Times

Harry Potter and the
  Sorcerer's Stone

Heart of Darkness

Henry IV, Part I

Henry V

Hiroshima

The Hobbit

The House of Seven
  Gables

I Know Why the Caged
  Bird Sings

The Iliad

Inferno

Inherit the Wind

Invisible Man

Jane Eyre

Johnny Tremain

The Joy Luck Club

Julius Caesar

The Jungle

The Killer Angels

King Lear

The Last of the
  Mohicans

Les Miserables

A Lesson Before Dying

The Little Prince

Little Women

Lord of the Flies

The Lord of the Rings

Macbeth

Madame Bovary

A Man for All Seasons

The Mayor of
  Casterbridge

The Merchant of Venice

A Midsummer Night's
  Dream

Moby Dick

Much Ado About
  Nothing

My Antonia

Narrative of the Life of
  Frederick Douglass

Native Son

The New Testament

Night

Notes from
  Underground

The Odyssey

The Oedipus Plays

Of Mice and Men

The Old Man and the
  Sea

The Old Testament

Oliver Twist

The Once and Future
  King

One Day in the Life of
  Ivan Denisovich

One Flew Over the
  Cuckoo's Nest

One Hundred Years of
  Solitude

Othello

Our Town

The Outsiders

Paradise Lost

A Passage to India

The Pearl

The Picture of Dorian
  Gray

Poe's Short Stories

A Portrait of the Artist
  as a Young Man

Pride and Prejudice

The Prince

A Raisin in the Sun

The Red Badge of
  Courage

The Republic

Richard III

Robinson Crusoe

Romeo and Juliet

The Scarlet Letter

A Separate Peace

Silas Marner

Sir Gawain and the
  Green Knight

Slaughterhouse-Five

Snow Falling on Cedars

Song of Solomon

The Sound and the Fury

Steppenwolf

The Stranger

Streetcar Named
  Desire

The Sun Also Rises

A Tale of Two Cities

The Taming of the
  Shrew

The Tempest

Tess of the d'Ubervilles

Their Eyes Were
  Watching God

Things Fall Apart

The Things They
  Carried

To Kill a Mockingbird

To the Lighthouse

Treasure Island

Twelfth Night

Ulysses

Uncle Tom's Cabin

Walden

War and Peace

Wuthering Heights

A Yellow Raft in Blue
  Water